Kew Gardens: Urban Village in the Big City

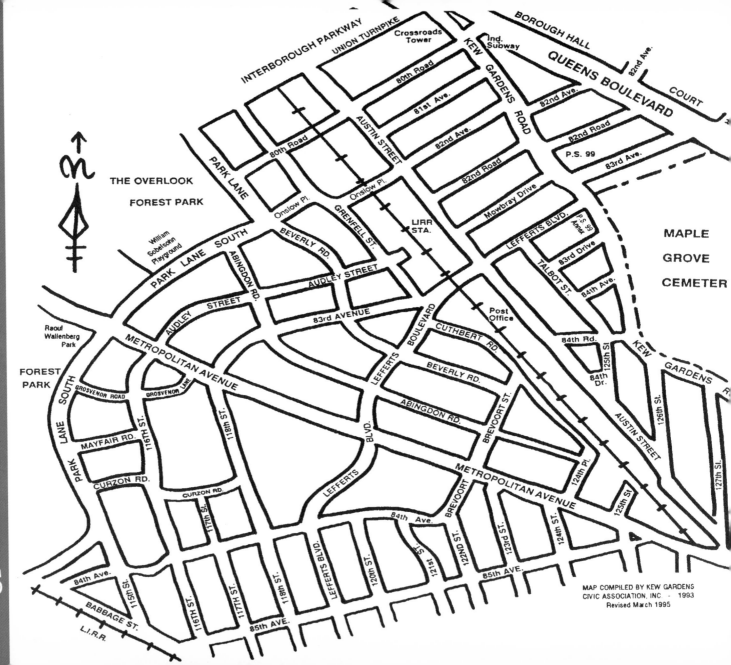

MAP
OF
KEW
GARDENS

THE OVERLOOK
FOREST PARK

FOREST
PARK

MAPLE
GROVE
CEMETER

MAP COMPILED BY KEW GARDENS
CIVIC ASSOCIATION, INC. - 1993
Revised March 1995

KEW GARDENS:
URBAN VILLAGE IN THE BIG CITY

An Architectural History of Kew Gardens

by BARRY LEWIS

Kew Gardens Council for Recreation and the Arts, Inc.
Kew Gardens, New York
1999

Published and copyright © 1999
Kew Gardens Council for Recreation and the Arts, Inc.
[A NOT-FOR-PROFIT CORPORATION]
105 82nd Road, Kew Gardens, New York 11415

Printed and bound in the United States of America

ISBN 0-9670954-0-9

FOREWORD

SEVERAL YEARS AGO, the Kew Gardens Improvement Association, Inc. (KGIA) sponsored an illustrated lecture by architectural historian Barry Lewis, a Kew Gardens resident. That lecture, at P.S. 99, on the architectural history of Kew Gardens was so well received that it was repeated "by popular request." Sylvia Hack, president of KGIA, then prevailed upon Mr. Lewis to "put it in writing" so that it could be published as part of KGIA's effort to have Kew Gardens declared a historic district and, ultimately, a landmark.

Since both the "book" and preparation for the historic district designation would require additional information, fellow architectural historian Harry Hansen was engaged to further explore and research the history of our community. Hansen's study was then fused by Barry Lewis with his own extrapolation. Many photographs were added to the original P.S. 99 presentation, resulting essentially in the manuscript and illustrations for the present book.

The somewhat raw computer disks were then turned over to Martin Hack and to Murray Berger (longtime president and chairman of the Board of the Kew Gardens Civic Association). They ultimately designed and production-edited the entire book, a long-lasting and dedicated *pro bono* labor of love involving countless hours on the computer.

In 1977, both men, along with Lois Wisnewski (then president of the P.S. 99 Parents Association) and Sylvia Hack had been co-founders of the Kew Gardens Council for Recreation and the Arts, Inc. (KGCRA), a "501 (c) (3)" not-for-profit corporation. It was KGCRA that ultimately became the publisher of record and coordinated the work and contributions of all who contributed to this literary and photographic endeavor.

Outside funding facilitated the project: first, a small grant from the Eliot Wilensky Fund; then, a larger grant from the J. M. Kaplan Fund to the KGIA at the research stage; and finally, a major grant from the Astor Foundation to the KGCRA, to go toward the printing costs. The Kew Gardens Civic Association has generously subscribed to the publication of the book as well. All of these funding measures plus the total commitment and untiring stamina of Messrs Lewis, Hack and Berger have finally made this book a reality.

We hope you enjoy this presentation as you read the text or skim through the expansive picture captions. Either way, we believe your perspective of Kew Gardens will be enhanced and enriched.

PREFACE

Across the United States, many once unique and flourishing towns and villages have disappeared. Many were lost as industries which supported them emigrated to developing countries, and the local industrialists who took pride in their towns were transmigrated into multicorporate officers with allegiance to no one and to no place. Other towns have been lost as a result of poor planning, developers' rush to gold, residents' naivete and indifferent political representatives. As James Kunstler's book, *The Geography of Nowhere,* documents, too many American "somewheres" have become "nowheres."

Kew Gardens is still a somewhere village. It is someplace worth saving, worth caring about and worth fighting to retain. For over eighty years, the people of Kew Gardens valued what they had and have. Now it is all too apparent that unless we achieve historic designation and recognition, the next generation may inherit only a shell of what exists. Kew Gardens will become a nowhere in particular, indistinguishable from other nowheres in our city, our state and our country.

Now is the time to seek landmark designation for Kew Gardens. Such designation not only places an architectural value on our village, it adds economic value and enables the fragile life of the community to be invigorated.

We who reside in Kew Gardens and have spent decades loving this community, know it to be an integral whole. But, like any whole, it is threatened with disintegration by destructive forces that must be reckoned with daily. New York City has managed to save but a few of its community gems. Too often city administrators have sacrificed neighborhoods by short-term thinking when the longer view would have been wiser.

Those of us who believe that where we live matters must fight for the kind of change as well as for the *status quo*, which adds to and preserves Kew Gardens. We don't believe that a community can survive as a museum. Neither do we believe that it can survive as a bland, non-distinctive nowhere, a clone of other faceless communities.

We hope that those who read this book will join with us to keep Kew Gardens the special somewhere it is, and help achieve the changes which make it a community that people do not flee from but live and grow in, now and for generations to come.

SYLVIA HACK

TABLE OF CONTENTS

Kew Gardens: Urban Village in the Big City

KEW GARDENS: URBAN VILLAGE IN THE BIG CITY

K EW GARDENS WAS BUILT by a generation that had seen the city and felt it did not entirely work. This was a cosmopolitan generation that wanted the culture and opportunities a city offered but didn't know why they had to put up with the nerve-wracking assault on the senses and the demeaning lack of personal space that came along with the urban territory. As Americans in this land of Transcendentalists like Emerson and Thoreau, they felt that subjecting oneself to an unending barrage of noise, crime, pollution and congestion was not conducive to the "pursuit of happiness." Cities needed to be dense for the exchange of ideas and people that urban life afforded, but when we went home in the evening after a day of such "excitement" we definitely needed respite: we needed the tranquility of a natural environment to calm our nerves and the anchorage of a solid community to offset the inherent social maelstrom of modern city life.

Lefferts Boulevard, looking north, c. 1940. The "downtown" of Kew Gardens showing "the bridge" over the LIRR. On the left, Tudor Revival stores sit on the "ponte vecchio," c. 1931. Background left: Mowbray Apartment-Hotel, 1924.

Urban villages

This was the underlying raison-d'être of the Anglo-American garden suburb, a concept developed in England and the United States in the mid-19th century and fine-tuned by the 1900's with communities like Hampstead Garden Suburb (1906) in London and Forest Hills Gardens, Jackson Heights and Kew Gardens (1910) in New York City. These garden suburbs would be leafy urban villages. They would be linked to the city's core by rapid transit and threaded with parks, recreational facilities, and community clubhouses. They would be communities where residents could renew themselves physically and intellectually and raise their families in a decent, natural environment.

The key word here is "urban." Today the term "suburb" conjures up images of tract developments, shopping malls, office parks and a life completely wedded to the car. But the pre-World War II garden suburbs were organized so that goods, services and mass transit could be reached by foot. The walkability of the community and its tight physical development encouraged the chance encounters and the mixing of different classes and cultures that are part of the urban experience. If America chose after World War II to abandon this model, it paid a price. It is not just the clogged freeways and increased pollution that have given a sour taste to the American dream; it is also the growing alienation of a suburban society that lives entirely in its "bubble," the automobile.

Life-in-the-car guarantees our insularity, but by living in our vehicular bubbles we are becoming a nation increasingly isolated from one another and, with that isolation, perhaps increasingly intolerant. It's a situation that calls for an alternative, one already given form by 1990's planners such as Elizabeth Plater-Zyberk/Andres Duany, Robert A. M. Stern and Peter Calthorpe. These professionals have created in their recent planned communities (Seaside, Florida by Plater-Zyberk and Duany is probably the best known) an alternative which has drawn the admiration and the praise of designers and city planners across the country. Yet these new communities are in fact an updated version of the garden suburbs of the early 20th century. For the "garden suburb" is an idea whose time has come back.

New York City's Planned Communities

Here in New York City we have the country's finest concentration of these early planned communities, reaching from Riverdale in The Bronx to Prospect Park South in Brooklyn. New York stretched the garden suburb concept to include all types of urban housing including high-rise apartment house complexes like Parkchester (1939), master plans for neighborhoods like the Upper West Side (1869) and working class developments, which include Sunnyside Gardens (1926).

Though New York is principally known for its dense, brownstone districts such as Park Slope and its grand apartment house boulevards that would include upper Broadway and Park Avenue, our city's architectural heritage is equally enriched by its cluster of garden suburb neighborhoods. Whether it's Jackson Heights or Parkchester, Tudor City or Forest Hills Gardens, New York City's

planned communities offer us American urban design that is both richly varied and highly instructive, giving us, possibly, lessons for the 21st century. It is this planning heritage that New York City's Landmarks Preservation Commission should begin to focus on, especially now that Riverdale, Jackson Heights and Douglaston have been designated Historic Districts, and Kew Gardens is considering the application process.

The Seven Sisters

Queens is especially rich in this heritage. Seven planned communities, "the Seven Sisters," were built over the course of eighty years with the first, Richmond Hill, emerging in the 1870's and the last, Fresh Meadows, around 1950. The middle five were developed simultaneously, if independently, between 1910 and 1930, and they include Forest Hills Gardens, Kew Gardens, Jackson Heights, Douglaston and Sunnyside Gardens. Each of these was developed by a different "builder," each offered a different mixture of housing, retail and community facilities, and each gives us a different variation of country-in-the-city, *rus in urbe* living. Sunnyside Gardens and Jackson Heights were more densely urban, Douglaston was more rural, while Forest Hills Gardens and Kew Gardens were a mixture of both rural and urban environments. As for motive, Sunnyside and Forest Hills Gardens were built as utopian experiments (with a limited profit!) while the other three were nurtured by private developers who were not shy about making money. These developers were shrewd businessmen with an eye for a dollar; they understood that a well designed "development" would attract a wealthier clientele and earn heftier profits. But obviously, in carefully honing the garden suburb ideal to their particular vision, they were looking for something else besides money: an alternative to the faceless, mass-produced monotony of the brownstones of the 19th century and the wood-framed tract developments of the early 20th.

The builders of all five communities were as varied and as interesting as the communities they built. They considered themselves the patrons, and patronesses, of a new kind of urban experiment and shepherded their growing communities, much as an 18th century English squire would watch over his model village. Certainly there's a story to be told in the lives of these creative people: the patrician Mrs. Olivia Sage (Forest Hills Gardens), the progressive team of Clarence Stein, Henry Wright and Alexander Bing (Sunnyside), the flamboyant, arm-twisting Edward MacDougall (Jackson Heights), the yachtsman William Douglas and the Rickert-Finlay Realty Company (Douglaston) and the close-knit brothers of the Man family (Kew Gardens). Each obviously knew of the garden suburb tradition, and each translated it for us in his or her own terms.

THE ORIGINS OF KEW GARDENS

KEW GARDENS' ORIGINS GO BACK to the 17th century and the founding of Dutch New Netherlands. In 1655, two years after the chartering of New Amsterdam on Manhattan Island, Rustdorp, today's Jamaica, was established on the flat plain of southern Long Island, just south of the backbone of hills known as the terminal moraine. The moraine, a product of the ice age, created a line of hills along the western edge of Long Island (now Prospect Park and stretching south to Bay Ridge), that turned eastward and ran directly through the middle of this 100-mile-long island. North of the moraine the terrain was hilly and the shoreline "fjord"-like with a string of picturesque bays. South of the moraine the land was flat and sloped gently towards the ocean beaches of the south shore. Rustdorp lay right between these two landscapes.

This dramatic difference in topography would affect the course of urban development that began in the mid-19th century. The south shore flatlands, mostly potato and duck farms, became working and middle class tract housing, though pockets of affluence developed near Hewlett Bay (the Five Towns) and out east around Oakdale. The north shore with its rolling, wooded hills and sheltered bays attracted the horse breeders and yachtsmen of wealthy New York, creating the Gold Coast that we know today. Kew Gardens would be part of that north shore development.

The English took over in 1664, renamed

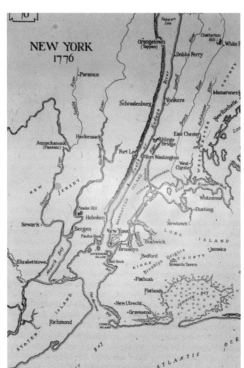

New York metropolitan area, 1776. On the right, in mid-Long Island, is Jamaica, founded 1655. To its northwest, will be built Richmond Hill (1869) and Kew Gardens (1910).

the entire colony New York and in 1683 divided it into separate counties whose governments and borders still exist today. Five of those counties would eventually be united in 1898 to form Greater New York: New York (Manhattan Island), Westchester (whose southern tip became The Bronx), Richmond (Staten Island), Kings (including the hamlet of Brooklyn) and Queens (which stretched to the Suffolk County border; its eastern half would become Nassau County in 1898). The latter two counties, Kings and Queens, were named for King Charles II of England and his wife, Queen Catherine of Braganza. The entire colony and its chief city, were named for the King's brother, the Duke of York, who would soon become James II.

The English converted the Dutch Rustdorp into Jamaica (from the Native American word for "beaver") and made it the county seat of Queens County. This was logical, as it was approximately midway between the East River and the Suffolk County line and lay astride the island's most important east-west route, the King's Highway. The latter was an old Dutch road that ran through the center of the island connecting Brooklyn (Breukelen) on the west with Jamaica and Hempstead, further east. Probably in its origins a Native American trail, it served for generations as the principal route for bringing Long Island's farm products via Brooklyn's East River ferries to the growing masses in New York City.

Development in the early 19th century

The King's Highway was "improved" in 1809 during the great era of turnpike building by leasing it to a private company that "paved" it with wooden planks, thus insuring against its becoming a quagmire in the rain and a dust storm in the summer heat. Though more reliable for travelling, this former public highway was now a private road, and the company charged tolls for those who travelled it — an early example of privatizing the public sphere. Its new name was the Brooklyn and Jamaica Turnpike; its attractiveness increased when Robert Fulton invented the steamboat and when the Brooklyn ferries went high-tech with steam engines in 1814. To honor him, the Turnpike was eventually renamed Fulton Street for its entire length, but the Queens section would be renamed again in 1918 as Jamaica Avenue. Whatever its nomenclature, the old King's Highway was a principal through route and when the railroad was built in the 1830's, it would follow roughly the same path.

A second modern road was built in 1814, the Williamsburg and Jamaica Turnpike, connecting Jamaica to the ferries at Williamsburg, Brooklyn's neighbor and rival on the East River (though Williamsburg eventually lost the fight and was annexed by Brooklyn in 1855). Today, that turnpike is known as Metropolitan Avenue. The latter became the northern border for the 19th century Richmond Hill development and eventually an important commercial and apartment house street in contemporary Kew Gardens.

A third important road in the vicinity, though never made a turnpike, was the Newtown-Jamaica Road or Newtown Road linking Newtown (today's Elmhurst) and Jamaica, joining the Jamaica Turnpike near what is now the Van Wyck Expressway. It basically was the forerunner of today's Queens Boulevard; however, when the road reached the marshland that is currently the Queens Borough Hall district, it avoided the flood-prone swamps by running through the hills that lay immediately to the south. Around 1870, with better

technology at hand, a more direct route was laid out, this time going through the marshes, and the entire stretch renamed Hoffman Boulevard in "honor" of one of William Marcy Tweed's political cronies. Hoffman Boulevard was absorbed around 1910 into the new Queens Boulevard, the latter serving as a main through-route to the just-opened (1909) Queensborough Bridge. The old segment of Newtown Road that ran through the hills was reduced to a feeder road and renamed for the new community, Kew Gardens Road.

The Railroad

In the 1830's it was considered impossible to build a railroad along Connecticut's spongy shoreline, so the backers of the Long Island Railroad (LIRR) assumed their line would be, along with ferries across Long Island Sound and train lines in New England, the main route between New York and Boston. The LIRR was built with the expectation it would be one of America's busiest railroads. But within a generation, technology improved. The faster all-rail line via Connecticut was possible, and the LIRR was condemned to a dead-end existence, yet one important for the island it served. The railroad's first "city" terminal was at the East River and Atlantic Avenue (south of today's Brooklyn Heights) where ferries took its cargo and commuters to Manhattan's shores, and its tracks ran eastward down the center of Atlantic Avenue all the way to Jamaica (1836), continuing on to Hicksville (1837) and to Montauk (1844), its roadbed roughly paralleling the Jamaica Turnpike's route.

As Brooklyn grew (it became a City in 1835 and was slowly annexing the other towns of Kings County), it found the railroad's right-of-way a nuisance causing countless accidents and deaths along the Atlantic Avenue route. (For the same reason, New York's Eleventh Avenue became known as "Death Avenue"; its crowded streets, nervous horses and noisy, smoky locomotives could not co-exist.) By the Civil War era, Brooklyn decided the railroad had to go. The LIRR bought land for a new Main Line to the East River via the more rural, and therefore less problematic, Queens County. In 1861 a new East River terminal at Hunters Point (Queens) was built so ferries could take the new line's passengers to downtown New York. Ironically, seventy years later the city built its first vehicular tunnel between Long Island and New York at approximately the same point, with the toll booths of the Queens-Midtown Tunnel only yards from the old decaying ferry piers.

Early developments follow the railroad

This re-aligned rail route opened the rural precincts of Queens County to new urban developments, the first of which were naturally located near Jamaica, the County's major town and principal seat. The growth of Jamaica after the Civil War as a bustling county seat, the laying out of Richmond Hill as a garden suburb in the 1870's and the creation of Woodhaven as a factory town in the 1890's would all lie in the old King's Highway corridor.

A curious early effort at development was Silas Butler's purchasing in 1835 of a triangle of farms north of Jamaica Turnpike where the Newtown Road joined it. That area, immediately east of today's Kew Gardens, was sub-divided into 1,032 lots, though nothing much was built until the early 20th century. The lots were narrow and deep, laid out along a strict grid system of streets, and there were no controls over development. When finally built up in the 1910's and '20's and informally called "Haystown" after one of the early farms, the houses were simple wood frame constructions that architectural historian Alan Gowans has called the working class "temple-front" house. Jammed together on small lots with little more than a driveway between them, with no provision for playing sports or taking solitary walks on a wooded pathway, no community clubhouse for social events and no town center for a focal point, this was the basic mass-produced tract development of the Civil War-to-World War II period. The lack of imagination in planning and lack of controls to guide development taught later real estate entrepreneurs, like the Mans and Mrs. Russell Sage, that if they wanted to create a quality community they had to do some serious thinking about planning, architectural overview and restrictive covenants that would control growth.

The railroad's new main line and ferry service were the infrastructure needed to persuade New York lawyer Albon Man to buy up, by 1869, five old farmsteads north of the Jamaica Turnpike just northwest of Jamaica and right where the new railroad line spun off from the old Brooklyn-bound route. The farms, including the Lefferts, the Bergen, the Welling, the Robertson and the Hendrickson estates, had been in their families' hands for generations. The Man tract swept up gently from the Jamaica Turnpike (Jamaica Avenue), broke into the hills of the moraine just south of the Williamsburg Turnpike (Metropolitan Avenue) and ended on the north at the old hilltop through-route, Newtown Road (Kew Gardens Road). The Man tract ran between Jamaica and Metropolitan Avenues from about 104th Street on the west to about 123rd Street on the east. North of Metropolitan Avenue it ran from today's Union Turnpike and Forest Park east to Lefferts Avenue (now, Boulevard). In later years, farms east of Lefferts Boulevard between Metropolitan Avenue and Maple Grove Cemetery were also purchased, extending the Man domain to the old Silas Butler tract. With the land bought, the stage was set for Richmond Hill to be nurtured into existence.

RICHMOND HILL

RICHMOND HILL WAS CONCEIVED in an era of unparalleled prosperity and growth. The Civil War was over and the victorious industrialized North could expand without hindrance. In the next thirty years the American economy boomed continuously, except for minor recessions and the not-so-minor stock market crash of 1873 and ensuing Depression of 1873-77. By the 1890's, America had emerged as the premier industrial power in the world.

During this period, American cities grew geometrically, especially New York (which, until 1874, included only Manhattan Island) whose population of 816,000 in 1860 had expanded to almost 1,500,000 by 1890. This mushrooming growth created such a crush for living space that the city reached across the Harlem River and grabbed the southern tip of Westchester in two bites in 1874 and 1894. At the other end, the city co-operated with the City of Brooklyn in the building of the Brooklyn Bridge to tap the rural farmlands of Kings County for future expansion.

It was not just space that New York's middle class was looking for. It was also a better quality of life. Americans of the 19th century believed, as did their English forebears, that the only proper place to raise a

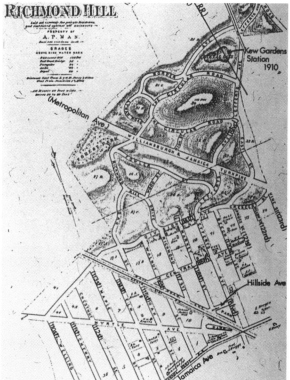

Map of Richmond Hill, 1874. Below Metropolitan Avenue, the "town" and the "village" center at Lefferts and Jamaica Avenues; above Metropolitan Avenue, the Richmond Hill Country and Golf Club (1895), later the site of Kew Gardens.

family was in a private house. Apartment house living was considered uncivilized, slightly immoral and fit only for the people of "foreign" countries, like France. But Manhattan's inflated real estate caused middle class houses to be jammed together, shrinking in width on smaller and smaller plots. Brownstone houses lined street after street, creating, according to Edith Wharton in *A Backward Glance*, a "cramped horizontal gridiron of a town without towers, porticoes, fountains or perspectives, hidebound in its deadly uniformity of mean ugliness." There were no squares or plazas, few parks and no "village halls" to serve as centers of community life. There were just brownstone rowhouses that went on endlessly: no sense of "neighborhood," no sense of "place" and a community whose spirit seemed as moribund as the brownstone fronts themselves.

This kind of faceless metropolitan expansion afflicted all industrialized cities from London to Chicago, and it was for this reason enlightened planners and designers turned to the "garden suburb" ideal as a sane alternative. Here in the New York area Llewellyn Park, near West Orange, New Jersey was laid out by A. J. Davis in 1852 (though it lacked a town center), Garden City on Long Island was laid out by department store magnate A. T. Stewart in 1869, but probably the most sophisticated garden suburb of that time was Riverside, Illinois, outside of Chicago, designed by Frederick Law Olmsted in 1869. Riverside had a town center with a hotel, a railroad station and commercial buildings, a central park strung along both banks of the Des Plaines River, subsidiary neighborhood parks and an organic street plan that respected the natural topography; Chicago's Loop was only twenty minutes away, accessible by both railroad and a "parkway," the latter having been designed but never built. It was against this background of planned communities and ideal suburbs that the Man family developed Richmond Hill.

Albon Man and Edward Richmond

Albon Platt Man (1811-1891) lived on East 37th Street in New York's fashionable Murray Hill section and summered in Lawrence, Long Island. On his way to his summer place, as he rode along the Jamaica Turnpike, he probably noticed the property he would eventually purchase to create his community, Richmond Hill. The ultimate purchase of the land in 1869 and his conception of the community were likely due to the excellent advice of a talented local landscape architect by the name of Edward Richmond. We know little about Richmond (we don't even know what he looked like), but he was apparently aware of the latest thinking in garden suburb planning and perhaps set Man off in the right direction. Richmond died just as the project was beginning, and Man brought down Oliver B. Fowler, a real estate man from Nova Scotia, to help see the project through, but apparently Richmond was given the credit for the new suburb's inspiration. A circa 1922 Long Island Railroad promotional brochure touted the community as ". . .Richmond designed. . ." with ". . .streets and vistas of this first 'garden city' near New York. . . ." Man called his new community Richmond Hill and though it might have been named in honor of the deceased landscape architect, it is more likely that Man, an Anglophile, named it after the royal London suburb of Richmond-on-Thames whose Tudor palace had been a favorite lodging place for Henry VIII and Elizabeth I.

Richmond Hill was developed over the next forty years, with Man's sons taking over for him after his death in 1891. Man concentrated on developing the hub area near the Richmond Hill LIRR Station where a commercial area evolved, though it is unclear how much of that village center was due to Man and how much was part of an earlier settlement named Clarenceville. He carefully planned for the first homes to go up near the hub and then radiate northwards towards the hills of the moraine. His intent was to develop the easier and more convenient flatland first and then figure out what to do about the more difficult and more remote "hill country" later. Where the flat land erupted into hills, he laid out an east-west street he named Division Street (later called St. Ann's Avenue and today, 84th Avenue) keeping the new community below Division Street, while above it he laid out (or at least mapped out) wandering roads that meandered through the hilly terrain. It is this northern part of the Man property that eventually became Kew Gardens.

Albon Man understood that good planning makes for a good development, and that in turn attracts the "right kind" of people. He followed that principle in developing Richmond Hill, and his sons followed and refined it in the later development of Kew Gardens. There was no public zoning; New York would not adopt the nation's first zoning code until 1916. The Mans used restrictive covenants to dictate such items as site planning to insure uniform setbacks; front yard fences were forbidden, thereby insuring each street a greenbelt of lawns and gardens. In Richmond Hill, Man donated land for its school, its church, Church of the Resurrection on Church Street (today's 118th Street), and a village common surrounding the railroad station. The common's southern half was eventually buried under commercial development, but its northern half was retained and in 1904 became the site for a Carnegie-funded public library. The library's interior would be graced in 1938 with painter Philip

Evergood's classic WPA mural *The Story of Richmond Hill*. Man also constructed a water tower, still in use, in the hills of the moraine on what is today Audley Street, so that his residents would have that necessity of modern urban life, a good water system.

Maple Grove Cemetery

The only other "development" in the area was the laying out of Maple Grove Cemetery on the crest of one of the moraine's highest hills, northeast of the Man property on the other side of the Newtown Road. Maple Grove was conceived in the "new" tradition

Maple Grove Cemetery Gatehouse, c. 1880. The Victorian Picturesque on one of Kew Gardens' highest hills; an "inland" cemetery accessed by a railroad instead of funeral barges.

of romantic cemeteries begun at Mt. Auburn in Boston (1831) and introduced to the New York area with Green-Wood Cemetery in Brooklyn (1840). Before Central Park (1857) and the late 19th cen-

tury urban park movement (nearby Forest Park, opened in 1896, was part of that era), these romantically landscaped cemeteries were seen as verdant retreats from the newly industrializing city. Unlike our own time, Victorians more readily accepted death as simply a part of life and saw nothing macabre in picnicking, hiking or reading among the tree-shaded gravestones. It's interesting that Kew Gardens has at its western and northern borders examples of both 19th century solutions to dense urban sprawl, the romantic cemetery and the Olmstedian "central park."

Furthermore, Maple Grove is an early example of the inland cemeteries of the railroad era. Earlier cemeteries catering to urban folk were located near water so the funeral barges could deliver the bodies from the city. Green-Wood was built near the bay and Calvary in Queens was developed near Newtown Creek. But the railroad freed the burial grounds from waterside sites and Maple Grove was opened in 1875, shortly after the LIRR's Main Line came through. Its Superintendent's House, still facing the crest of Lefferts Boulevard at Kew Gardens Road, was built in 1880. For more efficient service the railroad built a branch line the same year to serve Maple Grove. Its original station was near Union Turnpike and Hoffman (Queens) Boulevard, but in 1895 a newer, more convenient Maple Grove Station was opened just west of Lefferts Boulevard, with New York City Police Commissioner Theodore Roosevelt in attendance. That line, which was replaced in 1910 by the new electrified Main Line, ran between Newtown (Kew Gardens) Road and today's Austin Street. Homeowners along the old right-of-way still find remnants of the trackage on their properties in the form of cinders and iron spikes.

The maturing of Richmond Hill

When Albon Man died, his three sons Alrick, Albon Jr. and Frederick took over the shepherding of Richmond Hill, thus further

LIRR depot, Richmond Hill, at Lefferts, Jamaica and Hillside Avenues, late 19th century. Richmond Hill's lifeline to "the city" (1861-1910) is today's non-electrified Montauk branch.

ensuring the development's prestigious character. Alrick pushed to incorporate Richmond Hill as an independent town and became its

A Richmond Hill street, c. 1900. Houses uniformly set back, open lawns unencumbered by fences and street trees planted by the Man family gave the claustrophobic city dweller an instant sense of space, sky and tranquility.

A Queen Anne style house, Richmond Hill, 1880's/1890's. The signature style of Richmond Hill is the American Queen Anne (or Shingle Style).

Detail of the gable. Simple architectural elements elegantly handled show the new professional training of late 19th century American architects.

first (and probably only) Village President in 1892. Shortlived, the town would be absorbed in 1898 with the rest of Queens into Greater New York. That annexation was favorably looked upon by the Man brothers, as it meant the extension of city services such as water and sewers, new rapid transit lines, and new bridges across the East River. All of these served to make Richmond Hill more desirable.

In 1894 the Mans co-operated with the City of Brooklyn in setting aside 536 acres of the wooded moraine hills as a new public greensward known as Forest Park. The park included fourteen acres donated by the Mans and fourteen acres donated by the Backus brothers whose land would soon be bought by Cord Meyer for the development of Forest Hills. These land owners understood that a nearby "central park" could only increase the value of their remaining real estate holdings as well as serve as a greenbelt/buffer against the urban sprawl of the nearby City of Brooklyn. The idea of setting aside large parks to serve as a "country refuge" for residents of nearby urban neighborhoods had become popular since Frederick Law Olmsted and Calvert Vaux built New York's Central Park in the 1850's and Brooklyn's Prospect Park a decade later. In Brooklyn the planners were able to create an entire greenbelt that began on the shores of the Atlantic Ocean at Coney Island, ran north along Ocean Parkway, through Prospect Park and east along the terminal moraine via Eastern Parkway to the Brooklyn city line at Bushwick. Olmsted and Vaux envisioned extending that greenbelt eastward into Queens County, so the creation of Forest Park in the 1890's was very much within the Olmsted and Vaux legacy. The new park would serve future city residents as their own slice of countryside where they could exercise, socialize, meditate or just plain relax. To serve those purposes, Forest Park included hiking and equestrian trails, tennis courts and a public golf course whose handsome 1904 shingle-styled Clubhouse by New York architects Herts & Tallent (architects of the Brooklyn Academy of Music and the New Amsterdam Theater) was recently restored in 1992.

Spring-fed Crystal Lake, Richmond Hill Country Club golf course, c. 1900. Today the site of the Kew Gardens LIRR Station. Running through the photo's center is Lefferts Avenue (Boulevard) the eastern edge of both the golf course and the original 1869 Man tract.

The Man brothers also created in the early 1890's a private golf course for their Richmond Hill residents in the hilly tract north of Metropolitan Avenue and then established a private tennis club adjacent to the golf course, around what is now Audley Street. One of the topographical features of the new golf course was a spring-fed pond called Crystal Lake on the northern tier of the property surrounded by the tree-dotted hills of the moraine. The Man brothers understood, like their father, that such hilly land was difficult to develop and, far from the railroad station, would be less desirable to live in. The Richmond Hill Country Club with its new Clubhouse (1892), golf course and tennis club would give the town's residents another good reason for living there, while it provided beneficial use of otherwise idle land that might one day be turned into buildable real estate. Edward MacDougall would follow the same policy later in Jackson Heights. Shrewd as they were, neither the Mans nor

Clubhouse of the Richmond Hill Golf and Country Club, c. 1895. When the 1910 LIRR Main Line bisected the RHCC and its golf course became Kew Gardens, this clubhouse was converted to a private home and moved to present-day Audley Street.

MacDougall gave up title to the land under their "country clubs" so they could always exercise the option of developing it. Little did the Mans, or Richmond Hill's residents, realize in 1895 how fast that development would come.

In 1910 the Long Island Railroad rebuilt and electrified its Main Line. The change that fostered the new development was the construction of Manhattan's Pennsylvania Station and the East River Tunnel which provided direct access from Queens. This was all made possible by the takeover of the LIRR by the powerful Pennsylvania Railroad in 1901. The electrification required a new Main Line alignment between Long Island City and Jamaica, one that would run through the grounds of the Richmond Hill Country Club, literally bisecting Crystal Lake. Suddenly, the golf course land was only sixteen minutes from midtown Manhattan and too valuable

for mere putting. The Clubhouse, barely eighteen years old, was closed down, moved and turned into a private home which sits today at 131 Audley Street. Golfers who were evicted from the Richmond Hill course re-grouped and built another private club on the east side of Flushing Meadows: the Queens Valley Golf Club. It opened in 1919; only it, too, like its predecessor, would last only twenty years. In 1939 developers, extending metropolitan New York further east, bought it to build the community of Kew Gardens Hills.

The Man family allowed the railroad to cut through their property, provided that a new station would be built; this would obviously be the nexus for a new development. They originally hoped to call this new community North Richmond Hill. However, they bowed to the will of the LIRR, which did not want the new station's name to

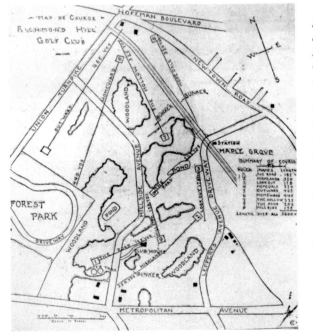

Map of golf course, Richmond Hill Golf and Country Club, c. 1906. Bordered by Union Tpke. and Forest Park on the west, Metropolitan Ave. on the south, Newtown (Kew Gardens) Rd. on the north and Lefferts Avenue (Blvd.) on the east. Note at the top, Hoffman Blvd., today's Queens Blvd.

be confused with the older Richmond Hill station only a few blocks to the south and instead proposed the name "Kew." The name was again derived from an English precedent, the Royal Botanical Gardens at Kew, next to Richmond-on-Thames. The Kew Gardens station was opened in 1910 on what had been only recently the pristine and hill-framed site of Crystal Lake.

KEW GARDENS: THE EARLY YEARS

I N 1912 THE SONS OF ALBON MAN set about to turn their country club land into a new community. That year they formed the Kew Gardens Corporation and transferred the privately held land their father had purchased back in 1869 to the new corporation. But this new corporate entity was truly a family affair. Alrick H. Man became the president, Arthur Man was named assistant secretary and Albon P. Man was the engineer of record on all of the maps the company filed. And as new opportunities arose, the Mans formed new corporations with a slight variation of corporate officers. Through these devices the brothers during the course of the next twenty-four years developed a profit-making residential development that incorporated the latest ideas in city planning. Possible influences on them were the recently completed London development, Hampstead Garden Suburb (1905), and perhaps the 1910 plan by Grosvenor Atterbury and the Olmsted brothers (sons of Frederick Law Olmsted of Central Park fame) for Mrs. Russell Sage's Forest Hills Gardens.

However, the plans for the Mans' "new town" were apparently not sketched out in detail in 1910 as were those for Mrs. Sage's development next door. Kew Gardens was not "created"; rather, it evolved over a generation as a combination of the Mans' enlightened ideas and their equally strong desire to turn a profit. Only a few miles to the west

Alrick Man (d. 1934), the "squire" of Kew Gardens. His father, Albon Man, built Richmond Hill and Alrick and his brothers Arthur and Albon, Jr. created Kew Gardens.

Edward MacDougall was also feeling his way towards a new kind of city neighborhood, beginning tentatively with quality New Law tenements in 1914 and culminating in the 1920's with the classic garden apartment towers Jackson Heights is known for. This incremental forging of an ideal with reality, this combination of shrewd business sense and enlightened patronage makes these speculative developments almost more interesting to study than the instantly realized plans and single-purpose idealism of the Forest Hills and Sunnyside "garden utopias."

Creating a community

As Albon Man had done in the earlier Richmond Hill development, the sons felt a good return on their investment was guaranteed if they invested in community facilities that would attract an upscale crowd. They helped establish key institutions such as the Kew Gardens Country Club, Forest Park, the community church (the First Church) and the local elementary school (P.S. 99). They built commercial buildings so that shopping would be convenient, reachable by foot and accessible by mass transit. Commercial activity was restricted to Lefferts Boulevard around the LIRR station and also to Metropolitan Avenue, which was a major road and trolley route to Brooklyn and New York. By erecting their own store

Pin oaks on Austin Street, looking west from Lefferts Boulevard. On the left, at the clearing, is the LIRR station. The Mans framed each street with pin oaks, now reaching forty feet, a neighborhood treasure in danger of disappearing.

fronts they not only could control the architectural detail, but they could also collect the rents.

They planted luxurious pin oaks along the sidewalks to give their streets a stately beauty and were probably responsible for bridging the LIRR at both Quentin Street (80th Road) and Onslow Place (82nd Avenue), in addition to the railroad's own bridges at Union Turnpike and Lefferts Boulevard. Whereas in most communities the railroad's tracks created a "Berlin Wall" between the two halves of town, here the community was not only physically knit together, but the residents north of the railroad had direct and easy access to Forest Park, while the residents on the south side of the railroad were convenient to the new main road to "the city," Queens Boulevard.

The Man brothers couldn't build all of Kew Gardens at once, so they sold some parcels to other developers but guided the devel-

opment through restrictive covenants. The Mans also laid out a street system that was cognizant of the topography, the existing main roads and the LIRR's right-of-way. North of the railroad they carved out streets whose names were alphabetically keyed to the old main north-south road, Lefferts Avenue (soon to be renamed Lefferts Boulevard). This nomenclature began on the east with Iris Place (84th Road at Dale Gardens), Juno Place (84th Avenue) and Kingsley Place (83rd Drive); then Lefferts Boulevard, and continuing on the west with Mowbray Place (now: Mowbray Drive), Newbold Place (82nd Road), Onslow Place (82nd Avenue), Pembroke Place (81st Avenue) and Quentin Street (80th Road). South of the railroad, running north and south across one of the area's most prominent hills, they laid out Park Lane (now Park Lane South), Richmond Hill Avenue (83rd Avenue, between Lefferts Boulevard and Metropolitan Avenue) and Audley Street. The latter two both reflect the gentle curve of Park Lane South and the border of Forest Park, and they give the Kew Gardens streetscape a more Olmstedian feeling than the rigid grid of Richmond Hill. They also served to give Richmond Hill residents quick access to the Kew Gardens village center and the new electrified Main Line station. The Mans saw Richmond Hill and Kew Gardens as sister communities and did not want the residents of the older neighborhood to feel slighted now that their rail line had been relegated to a non-electrified branch.

Also south of the railroad they laid out a second alphabetical group of streets, Abingdon, Beverly·and Cuthbert Roads and these have survived. It was City Hall's plan, slowly implemented from the 1910's to the 1930's, to impose a Manhattan style grid on Queens' patchwork of street systems that pushed the old names into oblivion. Some of the old street names and non-hyphenated addresses have survived. Those old names had character; certainly more so than the present jumble of numbered Roads, Drives and Avenues — and in fact were a good deal easier to remember. Many in Kew Gardens

Sunnyside Gardens, dual name street signs: modern number/original name. The old street names were an essential part of the neighborhood's character.

The "village" at Lefferts Boulevard, looking north from Beverly Road. On the right: modern awnings cover storefronts from the 1930's attached to 1920's Tudor Revival townhouses. At center: Tudor Revival "Homestead" building, stores and apartments, 1914. Left, above "Homestead" building: the Mowbray Apartment-Hotel, 1924.

would like to follow Sunnyside Gardens' recent (1980's) example and bring back the old nomenclature on new double-labelled street signs that would provide both the new number and the old name. This simple move could restore part of Kew Gardens' history.

The village

With the street system laid down, the new community could be developed. Over the course of twenty years a neo-Tudor village center, with stores and apartments-above-the-store, was built around the station with a modest but intriguingly original "ponte vecchio" carrying stores over the railroad tracks and re-enforcing the retail activity along the neighborhood's "main street," Lefferts Boulevard.

A neo-Georgian hotel, the Homestead (1921) was built adjacent to the railroad station providing local residents with a convenient place to house or entertain out-of-town guests. It was common

in those years for the other boroughs to have first-class hotels, convenient to the city, where tourists could avoid the expense and the tumult of Manhattan. Forest Hills Gardens' Forest Hills Inn, Brooklyn's St. George Hotel and The Bronx' Concourse Plaza, near Yankee Stadium, are only a few examples. Here in Kew Gardens the Homestead, designed in the style of a grand English country house, served as the community's "manor house," providing locals with a restaurant (in the days when hotel restaurants were considered the best eateries in town), ballrooms and an outdoor roof terrace for dining and dancing. Even through the 1960's the Homestead Hotel was known for the famous big bands it brought in from Manhattan, and on mild nights couples could dance on the terrace overlooking the "village" while the swing music wafted through the streets.

The Homestead Hotel, 1921, Grenfell Street, adjacent to the LIRR station. Kew Gardens' "manor house" provided the community with fine dining, elegant ball-rooms and dancing under the stars.

Reception
immediately following the ceremony
at
Homestead Hotel
82-45 Grenfell Avenue
Kew Gardens, N. Y.
1:00 o'clock

Please Respond

Invitation and wedding reception for Mr. and Mrs. Walter Eisenhardt, Sr., November 27, 1947 at the Homestead Hotel.

A second hotel was located on the edge of the community at Queens Boulevard and Kew Gardens Road. The Kew Gardens Inn (1920) was a residential hotel operated for family use with "special accommodations for bachelors." In the neo-Georgian style, again making reference to the manor houses of rural England, it had sweeping views of the marshy Flushing Meadows and the wooded hills to the east, some of which were home to the Queens Valley Golf Club. It had its own tennis courts and its residents/guests could use the facilities of the Kew Gardens Country

LIVE IN THE COUNTRY AT
Kew Gardens Inn
KEW GARDENS, L. I.—Only 15 Minutes from Penn Station

THE BEAUTIFUL NEW SUBURBAN HOTEL, DESIGNED FOR RESIDENT
GUESTS.—American Plan Only.
1 Room and Bath with Meals for One   2 Rooms and Bath with Meals for Two
$40 Weekly $85 Weekly
LARGER ARRANGEMENTS IF DESIRED. -- NOW OPEN
Under KNOTT Management
GEORGE H. WARTMAN, Manager   Phone Richmond Hill 3993

The Kew Gardens General Hospital, 1940, which had been the Kew Gardens Inn, 1920. The building was demolished in 1982. Inset from Queenborough Magazine, August 1920.

Club. It achieved brief notoriety when "Daddy" Browning, a fifty-something New York millionaire, brought his fifteen-year old bride "Peaches" to the Inn in 1926 to escape the crowds of curiosity-seekers and reporters in Manhattan. A year later, the jury on the much publicized Ruth Snyder-Judd Gray murder case — they were lovers who murdered Ruth's husband for his life insurance — were sequestered at the Inn while the trial was held at Queens County Supreme Court. The case was supposedly the "inspiration" for the movie "Double Indemnity." By World War II, the Inn had been converted into the Kew Gardens General Hospital and in that capacity served as birthplace of singer and composer Art Garfunkel. Demolished in 1982, it was replaced in 1990 by the twelve-story glass skyscraper that has given the community a new, if not appreciated, skyline.

The residences

Fanning out from the railroad station and town core, private free-standing homes ranging in size from cottage to mansion, townhouse complexes and apartment houses would fill out the community over the course of thirty years, some built directly by the Man brothers and the rest influenced by their vision. They and the architects who worked for them, and other developers as well, whether it was in Kew Gardens, Jackson Heights or Riverdale, deserve a belated recognition for their efforts. Only recently, the "garden city" architects of that era, men like A. J. Thomas, Robert Tappan, Benjamin Braunstein and Dwight James Baum have begun to be better appreciated.

Kew Gardens' housing stock is impressive in its variety of type, style and site planning, insuring a wide range of accommodations for people of varied incomes. Whether their motives were visionary or merely economic, the Mans decided this community would not be a Scarsdale or a Great Neck where strict limits on lot size and house type meant only the very well-to-do need apply. Though perhaps not the working class utopia of Clarence Stein's Sunnyside Gardens, Kew Gardens brought the civility of garden suburb living to "all" levels of the middle class. In accordance with these principles, the interior layouts of apartments, whether elevator or walk-up, and houses, whether attached, two-family or free-standing, reflect the modern preference for light, airy and informal living

Ralph Bunche house, Grosvenor Rd., c. 1925. Kew Gardens residences, whether free-standing home, rowhouse or apartment were swathed in greenery and set in gardens giving the community's residents a country retreat on a daily basis.

spaces. Single and multi-family residences were sited and shaped according to what we would call today "environmentally sensitive" criteria. And *every* dwelling — free-standing house, townhouse or apartment tower — is swathed in greenery: trees, gardens and shrubbery cloak the community in a natural quilt of color and texture. The allées of pin oaks the Mans planted, which today reach fifty feet, framed each vista giving every house and apartment tower a naturalistic setting.

The Overlook, Forest Park, 1940's; rear left is the Kew Gardens Terrace Apartments, c. 1927 at Union Turnpike. and Park Lane South. Forest Park (1895) was the community's own Central Park with wooded hiking paths, equestrian trails, tennis courts and a golf course to provide "rest and recuperation" for the harried city dweller.

The Kew Gardens Country Club, Nathaniel Vickers, 1916-1934, at Lefferts Boulevard and Austin Street, the neighborhood's social center. Front view, above, shows Clubhouse entrance on Lefferts Blvd. today the site of the Austin Theater; rear view below shows tennis courts, now the site of the Post Office.

The park and the Clubhouse

The generation of 1900 inaugurated the belief we still maintain today in physical exercise, fresh air and sunshine as an antidote to the stresses of modern life. The century's first president, Theodore Roosevelt, epitomized this new middle class interest in vigorous (would we say today, "aerobic"?) outdoor activity. The newspapers and popular magazines were filled with articles admonishing their readers to pursue sports and fitness programs and promoting outdoor activities such as tennis, hiking, golf and bicycling.

Enlightened city planners criticized speculative urban development for its lack of recreational and athletic facilities. Progressive real estate promoters like the Man brothers understood that their clientele, the young professionals of their day, demanded such amenities before they would pay top dollar for their homes and apartments. Progressive in their politics, this generation of "the 00's" sought to create a post-Victorian lifestyle that was more informal, more egalitarian, more physically active and simply healthier than their 19th century predecessors. This first generation of the 20th century preferred the breezy activities of the tennis court to the formal rituals of the old-fashioned parlor. In Forest Park one could walk, run, think, ride horses or play sports. The park was more than just a greensward or the ecological salvation of a wooded moraine; it was the venue for living the good American life. "Town" was where you made your living, went to the opera or dined at grand restaurants, but the "country" was where you really learned to come alive and renew yourself.

And, finally, as a center for social activities and community life, the Elizabethan Revival Kew Gardens Country Club (1916; Nathaniel Vickers; demolished 1936 and subsequently the site of the Austin Theater) was built on Lefferts Boulevard across from the railroad station. The land under it was donated by the East Richmond Hill Land Company, a second Man-related development company that owned the land north and east of the railroad station (today's Talbot and Austin Streets), which had been acquired some time after 1900. Once more, the Mans were shrewdly taking less desirable land, adjacent to the railroad tracks, and putting it to good use making the community more attractive and their investment more lucrative. With tennis courts at the rear (on the site of today's Austin Sreet, where the Post Office is located) and bowling alleys, billiard room, auditorium, social hall, restaurant, reading room and card rooms that could double as classrooms, the Clubhouse provided for recreation, social events and political meetings, giving the new neighborhood a central focus and a strong sense of identity.

In sum, Kew Gardens would be not just a "development," but a true community.

A COMFORTABLE LIFE STYLE

THE MAN BROTHERS' SHREWD PLANNING DECISIONS attracted a certain kind of resident. Like its sister neighborhoods in Queens, Kew Gardens in the 1910's and '20's became the home of film stars, theater people, writers and musicians. Times Square was quickly reached by the railroad (in the 1920's Kew Gardens was served by up to one hundred trains a day) and the Astoria Movie Studios, then the Hollywood of its time, was a short distance by car. Celebrities settled into this proto-Beverly Hills on "the north shore" that included Jackson Heights, Forest Hills Gardens, Douglaston, Whitestone, Bayside and Kew Gardens. In "Kew," as a local newspaper, *Kew-Forest Life,* constantly referred to it, residents included Charlie Chaplin who lived here between 1919 and 1921 in a small, "English-cottage" styled house at 105 Mowbray Drive. The very British Arts-and-Crafts detailing of the Chaplin house, its uniqueness for the neighborhood and the fact that Mr. Chaplin was its first occupant, lead us to assume that it was designed specifically for him.

Will Rogers also lived here during that period, primarily at 81-26 Austin Street, during which time his son went to the nearby Kew-Forest School. Other residents included Anais Nin, Joseph Mankiewicz, Charles Farrell, Gertrude Berg, Miriam Hopkins, Dorothy Parker and George Gershwin. In later years, United Nations diplomat and Nobel Prize winner Ralph Bunche lived on Grosvenor Road (National Register, listed 1976) at Park Lane South.

KEW~FOREST LIFE

Vol. 2 No. 37   Forest Hills, N. Y., September 2nd, 1931   Five Cents

Ruth Tara of Kew Gardens In Ziegfeld Follies, 1931

Ruth Tara, Ziegfeld Follies, 1931. Kew Gardens attracted the artistic middle class including actors, writers, artists, Broadway and film people as well as corporate types.

Throughout this period Kew Gardens apparently attracted the "artistic middle class" that today would more likely be living in places like TriBeCa, SoHo or the Flatiron District. Writers, artists, sculptors and musicians lived in the neighborhood, giving it a certain cosmopolitan and cultivated personality. In the pages of *Kew-Forest Life,* published between 1929 and 1933 and written in the breezy style reminiscent of *The New Yorker*, interviews with Kew Gardens residents attested to their artistic bent.

Life was sweet for those who lived here. Sixteen minutes from Penn Station and the attractions of Manhattan, the community was at the edge of the built-up city, allowing quick access to the resorts of both North and South Shore Long Island. The Rockaways, a solid middle class beach resort, was a quick drive across the rural marshes of Jamaica Bay and a little further east lay the upscale summer resorts of Atlantic Beach and Long Beach, the Hamptons of their day.

Closer to home were the two golf courses, the public one in Forest Park and the private one, Queens Valley, across the Flushing Meadows. Tennis courts were available not only at the Clubhouse and in Forest Park, but several apartment houses, such as the Crestwood on Iris Place (today's 84th Road between 125th Street and Austin Street) had their own private courts. In the winter, the Clubhouse courts were flooded for ice skating; in the summer, the Homestead Hotel had outdoor dancing on its terrace

Kew Forest Life *was a local publication covering the Kew Gardens and Forest Hills "scene." Issues included interviews with talented local residents who were often in the theater and other arts. Left: Cover, March 30, 1932, local young ladies as "The Dancing Dice" in the "Varieties of 1932," at the Kew Gardens Clubhouse; center: Marjorie Gateson, of Beverly Road, "well known stage star," interview November 23, 1929; right: Louis Persinger, of Union Turnpike, who was Yehudi Menuhin's teacher and an internationally known violinist, interview, April 26, 1930.*

overlooking the "village." And nearby was the Overlook for baseball playing, children's playgrounds, picnicking or just plain sitting and reading a book; a few steps further were the wooded hills of Forest Park for more rustic ramblings.

For nearby shopping, movie palaces, legitimate theater and nightclubs there was downtown Jamaica, whose middle class department stores such as May's, Gertz and much later, Macy's, advertised to the ladies of Kew Gardens that fashionable frocks and smart men's

suits could be reached in only five minutes via the LIRR to the Union Hall Station (Union Hall Street near Jamaica Avenue and now abandoned) in the heart of the shopping district. As an example of Jamaica's entertainment fare, the young Mickey Rooney and Judy Garland could be seen on the stage of one of the local movie palaces, the Loew's Valencia (1927; John Eberson, and now the Tabernacle of Prayer for All People) where the auditorium was designed to look like the plaza of a Spanish Renaissance town and atmospheric "clouds" floated across the sky-painted ceiling. Another kind of entertainment was mentioned in the "Nearby Theaters" column of the February 1930 issue of *Kew-Forest Life:* Werba's Theater in

Kew Gardens resident Will Rogers and kids. With the Broadway theater and Astoria Movie Studios nearby, Kew Gardens was an early "Beverly Hills" in the 1910's and '20's.

Charlie Chaplin's house on Mowbray Drive (1916, H.G. Outwater), an English Arts-and- Crafts "cottage" that is unique to the neighborhood.

downtown Jamaica was showing *Hot Chocolat* an "all colored review" that included singer Edith Wilson and, on the piano, performing his hit song *Ain't Misbehavin'*, Mr. Thomas Waller.

And the Kew Gardens residences, whether multiple dwellings or private houses, were considered first class in their amenities. The apartment houses, in particular, offered numerous services. Most had 24-hour doormen and some like Kew Hall had central telephone services with every apartment routed through the central board. Though we might think it quaint and outmoded by today's standards, the central operator acted as an answering machine, messenger service, message board, wake-up call, call-waiting service and, in addition, she could track down your kids if they were playing in a friend's apartment.

Some buildings, like the Mowbray (82-67 Austin Street, at Lefferts Boulevard), operated as an apartment-hotel (an old New York idea from the 1890's) providing room service meals, maid service, a ballroom for private parties and a roof-top terrace and pavilion for summer soirées. The Kew Plaza (80-40 Lefferts Boulevard) had a ground floor tea room and restaurant, described in the brochure as "an old English dining room," that opened onto an Italian garden. The public

Nobel Prize winner Ralph Bunche. His house at 115-24 Grosvenor Road has been listed on the National Register for Historic Places since 1976.

June 7, 1930   KEW-FOREST LIFE

Mr. and Mrs. Josef Lhevinne of Kew Are Artists of International Fame

Wife, As Well As Husband, Has Achieved Recognition As Concert Pianist.

By BESS PARSLEY

Mr. and Mrs. Josef Lhevinne, who have lived in Kew Gardens for the last seven years, are both artists of international reputation. Mr. Lhevinne is one of the foremost pianists of the day—one of the top-notchers in the musical world. Mrs. Lhevinne has also achieved fame as a concert pianist, and often appears in joint recitals with her husband.

Mr. Lhevinne has just completed a tremendously successful tour of this country, playing from coast to coast, and he has now gone to Wisconsin for the summer months. There he will be the guest of some friends who have an estate at Portage, and who have converted a water tower on their place into a studio which they call "Josef's Tower." It was in this tower that Mr. Lhevinne learned many of the beautiful pieces of his last year's repertoire. For the next five weeks, he will also be teaching the master class at the American Conservatory in Chicago.

He does not intend, however, to devote all his time to music this summer as he is also a sports enthusiast. He is particularly fond of fishing and motor-boating, and he likes tennis, golf, archery, and rifle practice. Astronomy is another of his hobbies.

Mr. Lhevinne started his musical career when he was four years old, began regular lessons at the age of six, and made his first public appearance when he was eight. When he was twelve years old, he played at a large ball given by the Governor-General of Moscow to which all the aristocracy and the cream of Russian society were invited. Among the guests was the Grand Duke Constantine, who was president of the Moscow Imperial Conservatory. The Grand Duke was so impressed by Josef Lhevinne's playing that he immediately made arrangements for him to enter the conservatory and to become a pupil of Safonoff who

was a professor at the Moscow Conservatory.

During the war, Mr. and Mrs. Lhevinne were interned for five years in Germany as Russian subjects. They came to this country after the armistice, and have made their home on Richmond Hill Avenue in Kew ever since.

Both Mr. and Mrs. Lhevinne teach at the Juilliard School in New York. Teaching at the Juilliard School they consider a great pleasure as all the pu-

At seventeen, Mr. Lhevinne graduated from the Moscow Conservatory with very high honors and a gold medal. Four years later, he won a prize

in an international competition in which thirty-five musicians from every part of the world competed. Rubinstein had established a fund for these competi-

pils have fellowships, and many of the most talented young Americans study there.

Mrs. Lhevinne met her husband when

A charming photograph of Mr. and Josef Lhevinne.

Kew Gardens pianists, Josef Lhevinne and Mrs. Lhevinne in Kew-Forest Life, *June 7, 1930. These well known Russian émigré musicians lived on Richmond Hill Avenue (83rd Avenue).*

could patronize it, but it also provided tenants with meals in their own apartments. The Shellball (Talbot Street) had a "social room" that could hold a hundred people for social gatherings, celebrations or meetings. The Shellball, like the Mowbray, had maid service and valet service and, like the Kew Plaza, offered in its brochure built-in refrigerators (much like a commercial kitchen's wall units) that were cooled by pipes of iced brine fed from a central cooling plant. Apartments were routinely equipped with wall outlets for the radio antenna so their occupants could enjoy the best radio reception, much as we today accept cable television wiring. And if you needed your car, you could call the community garage on Kew Gardens Road and one of the garage men would bring your car around to the front of your building while the doorman informed you it was ready.

Kew Gardens was considered a prime residential community. Most other such communities restricted their populations to white, Anglo-Saxon and Protestant, specifically excluding Italians and

Luncheon, Tea and Dinner at the Oriole Tea Room , Kew Plaza at 80-40 Lefferts Boulevard (Kew-Forest Life, 1929).

KEW~FOREST LIFE
VOL. I. NO. 20   FOREST HILLS, N. Y., JULY 19, 1930   TEN CENTS

The above picture was snapped last Sunday at Queens Valley Golf Club during the Husband and Wife Tournament. Left to right: Judge Frank Adel, Mrs. M. T. Langworthy, Mrs. J. P. Pendleton, Dr. M. T. Langworthy, Dr. J. P. Pendleton, Mr. M. C. Turner. Mrs. Frank Adel is driving.

Executive Committee Endorses Election Of F. E. Knauss

B. M. T. Fare Collector Robbed

Hold Up Men Are Caught

A picturesque feature of the Mummers Parade in Forest Hills on July 4th. The belles are Mrs. William Vitt, Mrs. Gulf Grant, Mrs. Maybelle Woodruff and Mrs. M. A. Van Nostrand. The cabby is Mr. M. A. Van Nostrand.

Neighborhood activities, summer 1930

Jews, who were then rising up into the middle classes. New York in the 1920's was a city in which a tidal wave of ethnic populations was moving out of the ghettos and into the old WASP neighborhoods

THE ORIOLE

LUNCHEON 12 to 2 o'clock a la carte

AFTERNOON TEA

Special arrangements made for Bridge, Luncheon and Dinner Parties

6 to 8 o'clock DINNER $1.15

Orders taken for Cakes and Sandwiches

Private Dining Room

ORIOLE TEA ROOM

Plaza Apartments 8040 Lefferts Avenue

Kew Gardens, N. Y.

Telephone Cleveland 8060

KEW~FOREST LIFE

VOL. 1, NO. 13   FOREST HILLS, N. Y., MARCH 29, 1930   TEN CENTS

Independent Subway construction, Kew-Forest Life, *1930. Opening of the Subway (1936) and Interboro Parkway (1935) and bankruptcy of the Kew Gardens Corporation (1934) brought an end to the Man era in Kew Gardens.*

around town. Horrified at this "onslaught," the WASPs re-located to exclusive new suburbs that effectively barred these ethnics from moving in. Such restrictions were legal and even underlined in real estate advertisements, and certainly Kew Gardens had its share. But apparently this community was already more open than most on this issue, and a number of Jewish families, among them Joseph Lhevinne and his wife, both noted pianists, moved in without too much of a fuss. One long-time resident recently noted that when her parents, who were Jewish, moved to Queens in the 1920's, they chose Kew Gardens over Forest Hills Gardens because they felt they would be more accepted in the former and could live more comfortably. Kew Gardens in the '20's evokes the image of cosmopolitanism, mixing artistic types and business people (the Bohacks of

supermarket fame lived at 82-45 Beverly Road, the Bulovas of the watch company lived on Mowbray Drive, and Fleischmann, the yeast king, lived at Beverly Road and Brevoort Street, where the Beverly House now stands), golf types and show-biz types, all enjoying a Jazz Age ambiance.

This seemingly gilded life ended with the harsh realities of the Depression and the movie industry's shift to Hollywood. The city's subway opened to Union Turnpike in 1936 (Eighth Avenue service first, then Sixth Avenue service in 1940) lessening the community's sense of insularity. The Country Club went bankrupt in 1933-34, and its Clubhouse was demolished a year later. The Interboro Parkway opened in 1935 creating a physical barrier between Kew Gardens and Forest Hills Gardens and making the apartments along Union Turnpike less attractive. The Queens Valley Golf Club closed

Jackie Robinson (Interboro) Parkway, looking east from Park Lane South, 1940's. Linking Kew Gardens to the world, the Parkway became a physical barrier between Kew Gardens and its sister community, Forest Hills Gardens.

by 1939, depriving many of the locals of a major recreational facility. Large apartments had to be broken up, certain services curtailed and even the local newspaper, *Kew-Forest Life*, disappeared by 1933. The Kew Gardens Corporation went bankrupt and the Mans relinquished further control over future development. Alrick Man died in his home at 83-45 118th Street (formerly Church Street) on May 19, 1934. Certainly, the "old timers" must have felt their community was gone. But Kew Gardens merely re-invented itself.

Kew Gardens in the 1930's became the home to a large German Jewish population that had fled the Nazi regime. These exiled Europeans brought with them a cultivated sensibility that continued the neighborhood's artistic traditions. The Clubhouse site was developed as the *art moderne* Austin Theater (1936, John McNamara) which for years, through the 1960's, was one of the few cinemas outside of Manhattan that showed foreign films. Near the LIRR station, in the early 1960's, a Greenwich Village-type "beat" cafe operated, and through the early '60's jazz could be heard not only at the Homestead, where Bobby Sanabria's Latin Band and Doc Cheatam's orchestra played, but in several other clubs in the area. One of these clubs, the Rumpus Room on 83rd Avenue, featured big bands including appearances by Count Basie, Woody Herman and Buddy Rich. This cultural collage is today reflected in the neighborhood's polyglot population as Lefferts Boulevard resonates with a score of different languages and non-Western dress. In the present-day Kew Gardens, a survey of the pupils at the local public school, P.S. 99, has shown that, typical of Queens demographics in the 1980's and '90's, the children come from some fifty different countries and speak over thirty different languages.

When the Man brothers went bankrupt, most of their records were destroyed, and, with those records gone, much of the neighborhood's readily available history was lost. But the Mans' influence continued, and still continues, through the physical infrastructure they built years ago. In every manner, from planning through architectural design and landscaping, the Man brothers had created a livable community that attracted, and still attracts people to this day.

*Cartoon of Kew Gardens'
Thyra Samter Winslow,
from* Kew-Forest Life

THE PRIVATE HOUSES

K EW GARDENS' PRIVATE HOUSES, built mostly between 1910 and 1930, are very much a part of that golden age of American home building that began just before the turn of the century and ended with World War II. This classic period of domestic design resulted from the confluence of two trends. One was the young American generation's desire for a "comfortable house."

"Comfortable" was a buzz word of that era that connoted a post-Victorian rejection of everything the 19th century cherished. Victorians led lives of stiff, domestic formality; they rigidly segregated men and women and were very much concerned with keeping the outside environment at bay where it could not compromise the sanctity of home and hearth. Their interiors reflected that mindset: stiffly formal rooms, cluttered and fussy decor, rabbit-like warren layouts, narrow proportions and heavy window treatments. The new, 1900's generation, mirrored in the popular images of the Gibson man and the Gibson girl, literally cleaned house,

Park Lane South at Grosvenor Road. One of the area's largest houses (1925, Slee & Bryson) exemplifies the best in the community's domestic architecture: Beaux-Arts Revival styling, garden suburb landscaping and an Arts-and-Crafts sensibility for materials.

throwing out this Victorian world of formality, darkness and rigidity. The turn-of-the-century generation preferred light, simple, open interiors that reflected the new informal, suburban lifestyle. Interior walls came down as domestic life became looser and more relaxed. Exterior walls came down as well through the inclusion of conservatories, sleeping porches and outdoor verandas, allowing rooms to open up graciously to exterior gardens and sheltering trees, an important element for people whose domestic lives now centered around outdoor activity. Simple interiors were not only psychologically lighter to live with, but they were easier to clean, an important feature in an age when servants were becoming scarce or non-existent. And "decoration" was seen as the straightforward expression of simple, natural materials rather than the cluttered hodge-podge of bric-a-brac, tacked on details and flocked wallpaper.

The interest in a "comfortable" house coincided with a second trend of the era: the professional training of the American architect. American architects of that period, the era we call "the Beaux-Arts Revival," were the first in this country's history to be academically trained in the rigors of neo-classicism. Though individual Americans had been returning from the Ecole des Beaux Arts since the 1850's, it was only after 1900 that it became *de rigueur* for all American architects to graduate from a Beaux-Arts program. This program taught them how to lay out interiors in which space flowed gracefully and rooms were well proportioned. These interior layouts were then expressed in exterior designs that were carefully balanced and well integrated, giving these homes a classic sense of serenity. Even where Picturesque (asymmetrical) massing was used, often preferred because it

"Tara" in Kew Gardens (1925, Arthur B. Lincoln). A rich variety of Beaux-Arts styles makes the neighborhood architecturally interesting and the houses distinctively unique.

Neo-Georgian house, Mayfair Road, c. 1920's. Naturalistic English-style landscaping gave the neighborhood a "country" look.

A "salt box" at Park Lane South and 80th Road (Quentin Street) c. 1920's. Recently restored, it displays the spirit of the original by using natural materials of varying textures and colors to form an "organic" collage.

expressed so well the middle class concept of domestic informality, the houses still achieved a sense of balance and well-being, the hallmark of a neo-classical education.

These young architects were also taught to simplify forms, surfaces and textures. Unity of material and simplicity of form were keystones of the Beaux-Arts training and this "less-is-more" approach allowed them to extricate themselves from the Victorian penchant for fussy detailing and "embroidered" surfaces. With their training in tow, they could translate for their middle class clients the latter's yearnings for a new, modern, "comfortable" house.

Development begins

As the new Main Line and the Kew Station were under construction, the Man brothers set about insuring that the new neighborhood would indeed be filled with "comfortable" houses. The restrictive covenants, first used by their father in Richmond Hill, would insure quality construction; only the covenants here in Kew Gardens went further and were more uniformly applied.

Manufacturing uses were prohibited, minimum setbacks from the street and side and rear lot lines were spelled out and a minimum value of $5,000 ($100,000 today) per house was stipulated. These kinds of covenants were becoming increasingly popular in suburban developments that wished to maintain a certain quality. The Queens Chamber of Commerce in a 1915 publication already cites them as a widespread practice: "An interesting feature of the realty develop- ment of Queens has been the progress in certain areas of restricted property and high-class sections built up entirely with one-family dwellings, ranging in cost from $5,000 to $50,000 each."

Development was quick in the new settlement at Kew Gardens. By the time the new rail line began operation in 1910 the Haugaard Brothers, a building and development company from

Long Island Railroad Station, Kew Gardens (circa 1910). The new community, next to Richmond Hill, was named for London's Royal Botanical Gardens at Kew, adjacent to the Tudor palace of Richmond-on-Thames.

Richmond Hill, had already completed four single family homes within ". . . one or two minutes walk from Kew Station . . ." The 1908 Hyde Atlas indicates four frame houses on the west side of Newbold Place (82nd Road) that might represent these homes.

By 1915, according to LIRR promotional literature, 233 homes had already been completed, of which about 60% can be identified as Kew Gardens Corporation lots. These houses were spread throughout the area north of the station (the city-bound side) between Mowbray Drive and Quentin Street (80th Road) and on the south side (the Long Island-bound side) along Grenfell Street between Audley Street and Union Avenue (Union Turnpike). Interestingly, the first apartment house to rise, in 1915, was the Kew Bolmer, erected at the intersection of Kew Gardens Road and Queens Boulevard, then the edge of the community.

Beaux-Arts training and the "comfortable" house

STREETSCAPES: As the houses went up, the advantages of the architects' Beaux-Arts training became apparent. Interior layout and exterior elevation were more sensibly thought through than was the case with houses of the previous generation. But the education that taught them to sketch out a molding or outline a gable also taught them how to design for a "streetscape." Whether it was a boulevard in Paris, skyscrapers around lower Broadway's Bowling Green or a suburban street like the ones in Kew Gardens, the Beaux-Arts system taught its students the importance of ensemble design. Buildings had to fit in, and be polite to the buildings around them. Individualism was perfectly fine, especially in this country of rugged pioneers and frontier settlers, but the social order also had to be respected. Though Kew Gardens' houses, and the later apartment houses, differ radically in style, type and scale, rather than being jar- ring or chaotic, their individualisms work beautifully as an ensemble with their neighbors. Gambrol, hipped and gabled roofs, Dutch

An Italianate house on Grenfell Street and its neighbor. Richly varied shapes, styles and materials make each house distinctive but a Beaux-Arts sense of harmony still prevails along the neighborhood's streets.

Houses on 82nd Avenue (Onslow Place). In this typical Beaux-Arts streetscape varied Picturesque rooflines, gabled, gambrol and hipped create individualistic silhouettes that still work well together as neighbors.

Colonial Revival porches and Georgian Revival porticos, Jacobean Revival brickwork and Tudor Revival "half-timbering" give Kew Gardens' streetscape a liveliness that is always interesting and sometimes surprising, yet each politely defers to the street and its vista. And vistas, in the 19th century tradition of the picturesque, are everywhere to delight the eye: streets off Kew Gardens Road have their sightlines "capped" by the houses and the railroad station at Austin Street; streets off Park Lane South lead visually to Forest Park; Park Lane South itself gives us a magnificent vista as it climbs the hill south of Metropolitan Avenue and curves east towards Curzon Road, an area old-timers called Corn Hill; Richmond Hill

Georgian Revival with hipped roof on 81st Avenue (Pembroke Place). Spanish tiled roof, stuccoed walls, chimney, wooden shutters and balustrade create an organic collage that superbly fits the English garden setting.

Four entryways to Kew Gardens homes. Variety in style, material and texture visually make this community the special place it is. From left to right: vine-covered neo-Georgian wood portico; limestone neo-Baroque broken pediment set into a brick wall in Flemish bond; English cottage with a brick arched front door, stuccoed walls and a wooden entry pergola; Tudor Revival with half-timber above, diamond-patterned windows and roughhewn fieldstone ground floor.

Avenue (83rd Avenue) and Audley Street bend at the curve of the hill giving visual delight as we climb up and over between "the village" and Metropolitan Avenue. Everywhere there are idiosyncratic one-of-a-kinds, yet all the different parts work together. No doubt this was the architectural expression of a society that sought variety without forgetting the underlying social ties that help us work together.

MATERIALS: This generation of architects also understood materials. Kew Gardens houses are mostly of frame construction based on that most American of building elements, the two-by-four. But the cladding or skin of the houses comprises a rich variety of natural and man-made materials, giving us a certain texture that feels comfortable, naturalistic and domestic. These architects followed the Arts-and-Crafts era of the late 19th century and absorbed British artisan William Morris' dictum of choosing simple materials and using them with respect. Morris, and his English architectural allies, Norman Shaw and Philip Webb, had shown designers that costly marbles and gold leaf were not necessary for good domestic design. Architects of the Kew Gardens period, though officially classified as Beaux-Arts Revivalists, were imbued with this Arts-and-Crafts sensibility. They used unassuming materials like brick, stone, stucco, shingle, tile and wood as an artist uses color on his palette. Natural colors and textures were used to make the exteriors of these homes collages of natural effect allowing them to blend comfortably with the lush "English garden" landscaping. These were houses that had dignity in their simplicity. It is this rich texture of simple materials that we are gradually losing as today's harsher, more plasticized substitutes replace them. Too often the original materials are ripped out

Large neo-Georgian on Onslow Place (82nd Ave). Single family detached hous-es vary from large mansions reminiscent of Westchester suburbs to small cot-tages for families with more modest incomes.

Tudor Revival rowhouses on Austin Street, (1927, Martyn Weinstein). These "anti-brownstone" rowhouses have London-style interior layouts for more space, light and air, staggered fronts for greater privacy, front gardens for rus-tic greenery and individual styling that makes each house distinctive.

because of ignorance rather than cost. The loss of this original tex-ture is a sad one and gradually, in imperceptible bites, it lessens the special character of the neighborhood and compromises its unique-ness.

SIZE AND TYPE: What is also intriguing as one walks about the neighborhood is the even more surprising variety of house size and type. Unlike so many other suburban developments of the time, in Kew Gardens the Mans built detached houses of every size, includ-ing two-family versions as well as attached single family rowhouses. Though we can't be positive about their motives, it must have been obvious to the Man brothers that such varied housing would attract neighbors of different incomes. A palatial neo-Georgian, 152 Onslow Place, stands on a hill south of the railroad while a block

Two-family houses on Grenfell Street. Adjacent to the LIRR right-of-way, these "semi-detached" houses, only a block away from mansion-sized neo-Georgians, add to the variety of the neighborhood's housing stock.

away two-family houses are clustered along Grenfell Street (82-11 to 82-29) designed to blend into the single family homes around them. Only a block further, on the other side of the railroad tracks, a fine set of neo-Tudor rowhouses adds to the mix. This 1927 rowhouse complex (82-04 to 82-26 Austin Sreet and 123 to 127 82nd Avenue) shows us how careful attention was paid to all manner of housing. They have staggered fronts for privacy, lushly landscaped extended gardens, clustered garages for the automobile age and London-style interior plans with central stairs and full-width rooms, all of which put the old New York brownstones to shame. One could say that the mother/daughter houses on Grenfell Street and these attached houses on Austin Street were built because both sites lay along the railroad tracks and were not suitable for top-drawer development. But elsewhere in the neighborhood we see other examples of this mixing.

The largest houses in the district were built on or near Park Lane (Park Lane South) when this grand avenue was opened in 1921, its 100-foot width a result of the Mans donating part of the right-of-way to the city and naming it for the famous street that borders London's Hyde Park. The family understood that a grand street fronting on Forest Park could only increase the value of their adjoining properties. In the vicinity of Park Lane, south of Metropolitan Avenue, are the handsome, palatial custom designed houses along Grosvenor Road and Mayfair Road. Adjacent to these largest houses is a charming, small neo-Tudor cottage at 116-18 Park Lane South (at Grosvenor Road). And next to the cottage, between it and the apartment house at the corner of Metropolitan Avenue, one finds a c.1927 neo-Tudor rowhouse complex (116-30 to 116-22 Park Lane South), designed with the same quality as those on Austin Street. This kind of mixture — mansion, cottage, rowhouse and apartment building — one would never see in the upscale suburban developments of the day. It tells us that the Mans, for whatever reason, wanted a varied community.

SITE PLANS: Another variant that enriches the area is the use of different site plans. Kew Gardens' real estate plots, mostly an

Tudor Revival cottage, Park Lane South near Grosvenor Road, 1920's. This small L-shaped cottage faces the street in a traditional suburban manner.

Tudor Revival cottages around a landscaped circle, Beverly Road near Park Lane South, 1920-1922. A charming break in the usual suburban grid, these were specifically built by the Man family.

eighth of an acre and measuring 50 by 100 feet (Manhattan lots are a standard 25 by 100 feet), are larger than the lots in the older development of Richmond Hill. More land meant more lush landscaping, a more rural sense of space and a better sense of the rolling, hilly terrain giving the newer community a look that was quite distinctive from the older one. Furthermore, Richmond Hill's houses were uniformly set facing the street in the conventional fashion, and though Kew Gardens' houses for the most part follow the same convention, in the newer community there were attempts to break out of the orthodox mold. In one instance twin houses faced each other across a landscaped drive, at 115 and 113 Audley Street, though the latter unfortunately was demolished in the 1980's. In another, a group of modest neo-Tudor cottages were clustered around a tree-filled circle off Beverly Road near Park Lane South. These houses, 82-16, -18, -20 and -22 Beverly Road, which form a "rustic" enclave, can definitely be traced through deeds to their mid-1920's construction by the Kew Gardens Corporation and its sister corporate entity, the Kew Gardens Construction Corporation. They show us that the Mans were always thinking of innovative ways to set the tone for quality development in the blossoming neighborhood.

INTERIOR LAYOUTS: Going inside the houses, we find the same kind of thoughtfulness in interior layout. Like other houses of this period, interiors in Kew Gardens open up to the environment in the manner of a generation that followed Frank Lloyd Wright's Prairie houses and Charles and Henry Greene's California bungalows. Rooms flow easily one into the other and gently arched openings separate rooms, articulating interior space without dividing it with walls. Stuffy Victorian parlors are replaced by the more relaxed and informal "living room," which, with the dining room, serves as the main public suite of the house. Glassed-in conservatories, often called sun-rooms or sun-porches, were sited to face the rear or side garden for privacy and to extend the living room, in the manner of Wright's Prairie houses, into the verdant surroundings; multiple out-

door terraces, especially adjoining the master bedroom, allow for easy access to the outdoors; and sleeping porches, glassed in as we didn't have California's weather, all followed that era's emphasis, and our own, on fresh air, exercise and sunlight. The Victorian penchant for dark interiors and formal lifestyles had been banished.

Architectural styles

As we walk along Kew Gardens' streets we realize that this variety of size, material, texture and site plan is most emphatically re-enforced by the rich variety of architectural styles. The houses in Kew Gardens were designed in various Beaux-Arts Revival styles that were popular between 1900 and World War II, though in a sense we still, in the 1990's, envision the classic American suburban house in these architectural terms. Here again, Kew Gardens establishes a separate identity from its older sister, Richmond Hill, and its contemporary sister, Forest Hills Gardens. Richmond Hill's streets, built up mostly between 1870 and 1900, reflect the Victorian Queen Anne (or American Shingle Style, as it's sometimes called) that was made popular by architects like Henry Hobson Richardson, and the young McKim, Mead & White. Exteriors of varying patterns of shingle or clapboard, picturesque roofs with eyebrow windows and rambling porches that wrap around the homes, are images that tell us we are in Richmond Hill. But as we go north past 84th Avenue (Albon Man's Division Street and Alrick Man's St. Ann's Avenue) and begin to ascend the hills of the moraine, the architectural impression changes. The universal use of clapboard gives way to stucco, brick or half-timber framing; rooflines shift to Dutch Colonial hipped or gambrel, Georgian pediments or Tudor gables often fleshed out with red or green rounded Spanish tiles. The entire architectural vocabulary becomes more varied and more eclectic, but always within the Beaux-Arts Revivalist idiom.

Part of this is due to the presence of different developers and

Italianate

Anglo-Japanese

their use of different commercially available house plans that were published by professional architects. A developer might buy four contiguous lots from the Man brothers (especially in the early years when more lots were available) and use a single plan, with slight variation, for all four houses. There is an interesting example of this in the Dutch Revival houses at 110, 112, 114 and 116 Mowbray

Tudor Revival

Dutch Colonial Revival

Neo-Georgian in brick with a Spanish tiled, hipped roof.

Spanish Colonial Revival

Drive. Or, a developer might use the plans in a mix-and-match scheme such as an A-B-B-A or A-B-A-B pattern for his lots. This can be seen at 112, 114, 116 and 118 Audley Street, where two spartan neo-Georgians are bracketed by two Dutch Colonials. In better quality neighborhoods like the one the Mans were creating, the same house plan would be used less frequently or would be purposely varied while a number of custom designed houses were interspersed with the "plan" houses giving the streets a custom-made look.

If different developers produced different sets of houses, the different architects, all now schooled in the same Beaux-Arts tradition, produced a deliberate eclecticism that ran the entire gamut deemed suitable for "suburban" living. Architectural firms practicing in Kew Gardens included Slee & Bryson, Walter McQuade, Louis Almindinger and Frank Quimby. For their architectural vocabulary neo-Georgian, neo-Tudor and Dutch Colonial Revival and

Neo-Georgian in white clapboard, gable roof, dormer windows and double-columned portico.

Craftsman were the predominant styles, but interpretations and variations are endless.

There are examples, as well, of Italian Renaissance Revival (80-83 Grenfell Street, with its handsome free-standing garage in the same style), Anglo-Japanese (84-62 Beverly Road at Brevoort Street) and a neo-classicized Queen Anne (118 Mowbray Drive, 1912, H. C. Rossell). There's even the "English Cottage" of Charlie Chaplin at 105 Mowbray Drive, unique to the neighborhood and so reminiscent, if in small scale, of William Morris' own Red House of 1859. Though its other sister community, Forest Hills Gardens, is much more famous and the latter's site planning by the Olmsted brothers is certainly more sophisticated, the houses of Forest Hills Gardens are resolutely neo-Tudor. By comparison, Kew Gardens' streets are a lively mixture of architectural delights.

These diverse styles were not merely disposable costumes pasted onto standardized plans. The different styles allowed house buyers to choose the ambiance of their home, thus expressing the individuality of their tastes. Some might prefer the formal grandeur of the neo-Georgian; others the more relaxed informality of the neo-Tudor and the Dutch Colonial Revival. The latter is represented by numerous fine examples in the neighborhood and deserves our closer attention. Though often thought of as only another Revival style, the Dutch Colonial Revival, in particular, was perceived as a style for our time. Based on the informal and simple local Dutch cottages of the 17th century, it gave us a sense of our City's historical roots while it provided us with a type of house, a northern European cottage, developed for the same kind of weather and the lifestyle we have in our American northeast. Ironically, that very

Dutch Colonial Revival, Kew Gardens, Walter McQuade, c. 1925. The Beaux-Arts Revival gave us this modern layout: (lower plan) 1st floor, on the left, living room/conservatory in its own wing, and in back of main hall, a family den; (upper plan) on the 2nd floor, a master bedroom with its own veranda and in the back, on right, a sleeping porch.

informality and simplicity of medieval Holland and early America made it the perfect expression for modern living. In many ways these "Dutch Colonials" serve as our East Coast equivalent of the

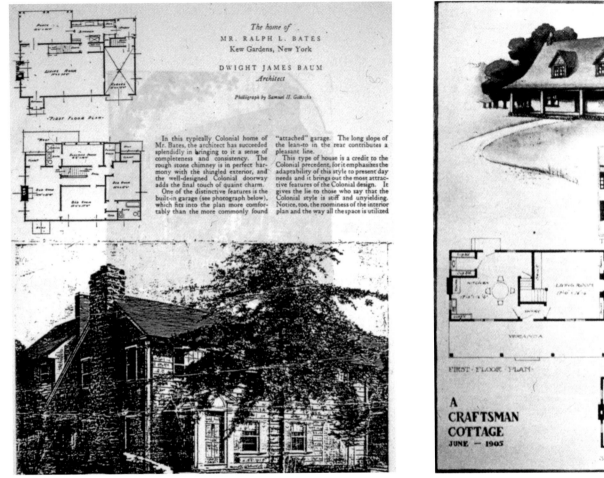

English Colonial Revival, 82nd Road (Newbold Place), Dwight James Baum, 1927. From Garden Home Builder, 1927. This superbly planned Beaux-Arts house has a single space living/dining room, a ground floor glassed-in conservatory (top plan), glassed-in sleeping porch on the bedroom floor (lower plan) and a rarity for its day, a garage integrated into the house.

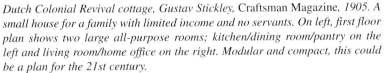

Dutch Colonial Revival cottage, Gustav Stickley, Craftsman Magazine, 1905. A small house for a family with limited income and no servants. On left, first floor plan shows two large all-purpose rooms; kitchen/dining room/pantry on the left and living room/home office on the right. Modular and compact, this could be a plan for the 21st century.

California bungalow. Designed for a minimum or no-servant age, the houses could be compact and, therefore, easy to maintain. Using the 17th century hall (a communal, all-purpose room that was the center of domestic activities) as a prototype, these houses sometimes combine living room and dining room to create one large, modular space in which furniture can be re-arranged at will, as was already mentioned at 99 Newbold Place (82nd Road), designed by Dwight James Baum in 1924. Baum, better known for his highly sophisticated designs for Riverdale and Manhattan's West Side "Y," here crafted from the 17th century Colonial Revival a superbly modern house built around a modular single-space living room/dining room that was modeled on the all purpose "hall" of the late medieval period. This "hall" is dominated by a rough-hewn stone fireplace and framed by spartan moldings, giving us a mix of an Arts-and-Crafts house interior and the openness of a modern day loft/apartment. Sometimes in these Dutch colonials the kitchen was combined with the living room/dining room space, much as it was in the 17th century, and very similar to the open kitchen plan so popular today.

Designer Gustave Stickley in his *Craftsman Magazine*, published between 1901 and 1915, often used the Dutch Colonial (or the Tudor Revival) for his craftsman houses, conceived primarily for people of modest means. Materials were kept simple and interiors were modest spaces serving multiple functions. Plans could be easily rearranged for customization.

In the restricted economy and changing times of the 1990's space is at a premium. Working couples share the domestic chores and the open kitchen is becoming the center of the home; the Dutch Colonial Revival, including its conservatories, terraces and sleeping porches (often used today as sunlit exercise rooms or home offices), seems relevant to the needs of our own coming turn-of-the-century.

Kew Gardens' houses, rather than being merely "cute" or "sweet," address the problems of contemporary life, showing us that these houses remain today interesting and instructive prototypes for modern domestic design.

THE APARTMENT HOUSES

KEW GARDENS' PRE-WORLD WAR II apartment buildings, like its private houses, belong to that golden era of residential design that existed between the two World Wars. New Yorkers had just begun to accept the apartment house when Kew Gardens began taking shape. The American custom of living in one's own private house had to change for New Yorkers when increasing land values in Manhattan forced the city's middle class into apartment houses, a process that began with a trickle in the 1870's and had become a flood by the 1900's. The upper crust still considered it a bit déclassé to inhabit one of those "filing cabinets for living" that lined upper Broadway, but by World War I the "Fifth Avenue crowd" had capitulated to the new way of life. After the Great War, with the rise of Park Avenue, nothing could be more chic, or more urban, than taking up residence in an apartment house.

Conversely, the apartment house was also one of the reasons why many of the middle class were leaving the city. These were the people who felt that living stacked one on top of the other was no way to raise a family. Privacy in the home was lost, communities became demoralized, traffic unbearable and breathing space rare and rationed. These profound changes, along with the even more disturbing tide of middle class ethnics that were sweep-

SHELLBALL APARTMENTS
TALBOT PLACE AT LEFFERTS BOULEVARD, KEW GARDENS, L. I.

Shellball Apartments, 83-00 Talbot Street, 1928.

ing over the old WASP city neighborhoods — it wasn't just the apartment buildings, it was "who" was moving into them — made for a huge exodus to the suburbs. This middle class flight was facilitated by the introduction of electrified commuter lines that made the journey downtown faster, cleaner and more convenient. It's no wonder that those who were moving to the new suburban developments had, literally, an "allergy" to apartment house construction.

Kew Gardens reacts to the apartment house

Though we are not sure of the circumstances behind the construction of Kew Gardens' first apartment house, we certainly can understand the reaction. The Kew Bolmer (80-45 Kew Gardens Road) was designed in 1914 for the acute angled intersection of Queens Boulevard and Kew Gardens Road at the edge of the new community. Like the nearby Kew Gardens Inn that would go up six years later, the Kew Bolmer must have been sited to take advantage of the rural views looking east over the Queens Valley (Flushing Meadows) as well as the Boulevard's new trolley line that ran via the Queensborough Bridge into "the city." Handsomely designed to fit the triangular site, it had balconies facing west, a picturesque cornice to delight those traveling east on the Boulevard, and surrounding gardens that today are buried under commercial storefronts. The nearby homeowners, who had just bought into the new community, were concerned. They organized the Kew Gardens Civic Association (1914) to protect against wanton incursion into Kew Gardens' residential areas as well as to provide for planned improvements — such as the foresighted insistence that utility wires be laid underground or strung in back yards where they would not be public eyesores.

The Mans, who considered themselves the "squires" of the village, found they were faced with a "revolution." Negotiations persisted over the course of a decade (World War I certainly must have interrupted the proceedings), but by the early 1920's an agreement was reached. The Mans, and other developers they might sell to, were forced to keep apartment houses confined to the main thoroughfares (Lefferts Boulevard, Metropolitan Avenue and Union Turnpike), leaving the side streets basically to single family homes. To this day that policy survives, re-enforced by current city zoning laws and the vigilant monitoring by the Kew Gardens Civic Association. It parallels similar contemporary attempts to limit apartment house construction on upper Fifth Avenue, culminating in 1921 in a seventy-five foot (about seven stories) height restriction on the Avenue from 60th to 96th Streets. But even the millionaires on Fifth Avenue couldn't stop the changing urban scene; the restriction was voided by the courts in 1924 and apartment buildings on Fifth Avenue opposite Central Park rose to the intemperate height of fifteen to twenty stories.

Similarly in Kew Gardens, the 1924 homeowners' "victory" over apartment house development was in fact a Pyrrhic one. Within five years apartment houses rose almost solidly along Lefferts Boulevard from Talbot Street south to 84th Avenue, along Metropolitan Avenue from one end of the community to the other, along Union Turnpike from Queens Boulevard to Forest Park, and even on scattered sites along 116th and 118th Streets between 84th and Metropolitan Avenues. These were not low-rise style apartment buildings. At a time when Manhattan apartment towers averaged about twenty floors, the new apartments in Kew Gardens, along with those in other borough neighborhoods, rose to seven stories, with the Mowbray, the Shellball and a few others rising to ten or more stories. They provided Kew Gardens an urban skyline and a more urban population; the homeowners would have to co-exist with very citified high-rise neighbors.

The Mans introduce apartment house living

The Man brothers' decision to include apartment houses in their new planned community is an interesting one, because it radically changed the nature of what the new community would be. Other upscale new communities like a Scarsdale or a Great Neck

The Mowbray (Benjamin Braunstein, 1924) under construction on Austin Sreet across from the LIRR station.

were composed strictly of single family homes with perhaps an apartment building or two near the railroad station. Suburbs were supposed to be exclusive and homogeneous with a low rise, leafy silhouette; apartment houses implied just the opposite. If the Mans were planning to put up numerous apartment buildings, they obviously had already decided that this would be a planned community mixing urban and suburban lifestyles. Rising land values in Queens may have had something to do with their decision. Sixteen minutes from Manhattan's Penn Station, Kew Gardens was almost too valuable a piece of property for "just" homes. Between 1910, when the Queensborough Bridge and the new LIRR both opened, and 1929, when the stock market crashed, land values in Queens rose over 400%; Queens ranked among the fastest growing counties in the United States. The Mans were too shrewd to let these facts go un-noticed and un-exploited.

The Kew Bolmer may have been on the edge of the community, but the Mans apparently intended to construct high-rise towers in the heart of their "garden suburb," near the railroad station where such densities made the most sense.

Though we may not be exactly sure of their plans, the brothers did play a role in the East Richmond Hill Land Company which owned the land just north of the railroad station as well as other lots east of Lefferts Boulevard, which was not part of their father's purchase in 1869; the Man brothers must have acquired this real estate after 1900. This land was apparently set aside mainly for apartment house development as well as the grounds for the Kew Gardens Country Club, all of which was being contemplated as early as 1915. The War and the Recession of 1919-1920 may have shelved their plans, but in 1922 the Kew Hall (83-09 Talbot Street) was put up at Talbot Street and Lefferts Boulevard, followed by the Kew Plaza (80-40 Lefferts Boulevard) and the Mowbray (82-67 Austin Street; Benjamin Braunstein) in 1924. By 1928 the East Richmond Hill Land Company property along Talbot Street was filled with apart-

ment houses, including the Shellball (1925-8; 83-00 Talbot Street), the Windsor Tower (1927; 83-52 Talbot Street) and the Parc Chateau (84-09 Talbot Street) capped at the eastern end by the innovative "town house" apartment complex of Dale Gardens. By 1929 over twenty apartment houses had gone up on the already mentioned main thoroughfares.

The garden apartment house

But if the apartment house was introduced into the neighborhood, it would be strictly along "garden suburb" lines. Queens architects, in the 1920's and '30's, were part of a nationwide movement that took the traditional European apartment house and civilized it in American terms. The "garden apartment," itself of European origin, offered an urban lifestyle and multi-family living, but swathed in the greenery of a peaceful, cloistered retreat. After World War II the term "garden apartment" was cheapened by the mass production of often tacky, low-rise, barely landscaped units. But the original complexes of the 1920's through '40's period brought a certain civility to city life that we today would do well to emulate. Greenbelted and garden-filled apartment blocks in Jackson Heights, Forest Hills Gardens and Kew Gardens, and developments like Boulevard Gardens (1929) in Woodside, offered a variety of site plans that gave city-dwelling Americans what they cherished most in their homes: the privacy of a single family house and the restful, recuperative setting of a country atmosphere.

And even densely packed Manhattan did not escape the "garden apartment" movement. New apartment complexes like London Terrace (1930) on West 23rd Street and the Parc Vendome (1931) on West 57th Street were built with interior garden courts, but the huge scale of the buildings, dictated by Manhattan's pricey real estate, subverted the garden city ideal. In Queens, however, as in the other boroughs, a European scale prevailed. Seven- to ten-story buildings

Original brochure for Beverly House, Beverly Road east of Lefferts Boulevard, Morris Rothstein & Sons, c. 1938. A superb garden apartment house on the site of the Anglo-Japanese Fleischmann house (of yeast fame, his daughter's house still stands across the street).

Kew Gardens Plaza, 80-40 Lefferts Boulevard, 1924. A classic Kew Gardens apartment house, confined to a narrow lot along the "main" street by the 1925 homeowners' agreement, it brought historic character, a greenbelt and an Italian garden (home of the Oriole Tea Room) to the restricted site.

allowed for light, air, spaciousness and greenery not attainable in the canyons of "the city." More reasonably priced land also meant apartment buildings did not have to be jammed together like books on a shelf with small air shafts for light, dark interiors and cramped alleyways for space. Kew Gardens apartment houses were designed as free-standing structures surrounded by belts of greenery (even if they were narrow ones) with landscaped courts of various shapes and sizes. They were truly "towers in a park" before that architectural sobriquet had come to mean "a brick box in a parking lot."

Apartment layouts and site plans

Yet apartment builders in Kew Gardens did not have large sites to work with, as Edward MacDougall did in Jackson Heights. Aside from particular complexes like the Kew Hall, Dale Gardens and the

later Kent Manor (now known as Hampton Court), the Mans and their builders had to work with narrow and confined lots. That didn't prevent the architects from applying their garden apartment ideals to whatever site they were given, proving that even on narrow lots of odd dimensions you could create garden apartments with multiple exposures, cross ventilation, a maximum of light and privacy — that is, if you cared to produce quality housing. To achieve this, Kew Gardens apartment house layouts and site plans took every conceivable shape. Perusing the Queens Historical Society's Thomas Hart Collection of original plans and brochures of 1920's and '30's apartment projects, one is struck by the infinite variety of building configurations carved out by Kew Gardens architects. Unlike the cranked-out plans of most speculative builders of the day, these apartment buildings were individually tailored to their different sites with various plans used to achieve the goals the Man brothers were after.

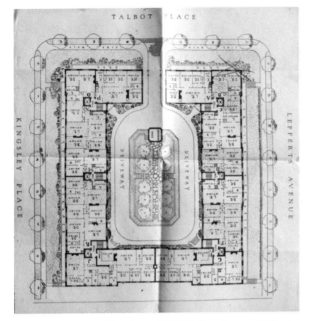

Kew Hall floor plan, original brochure, 83-09 Talbot Street, 1922. An early Kew Gardens apartment house, having the luxury of a large site, modeled its layout on Manhattan's Dakota Apartments. The original concierge's house remains.

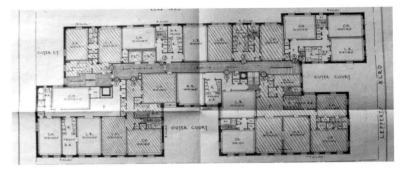

Shellball floor plan, original brochure, 83-00 Talbot Sreet, 1928. A "pinwheel" plan that exploited a restricted site for apartments that were cross-ventilated, well-lit and maintained their tenants' privacy. The different apartments appear shaded and un-shaded.

neo-Tudor garage building (most recently, a scale factory) for tenants' cars. The courtyarded plan appears in other Kew Gardens apartment complexes built throughout the '20's. The Kew Gardens Terrace at Union Turnpike and Park Lane South, the Forest Park

Mowbray floor plan, original brochure, 82-67 Austin Street, Benjamin Braunstein, 1924. Another example of the "pinwheel" plan for apartment buildings. This was originally run as an apartment-hotel though its guests were all "permanent" tenants, an old New York idea.

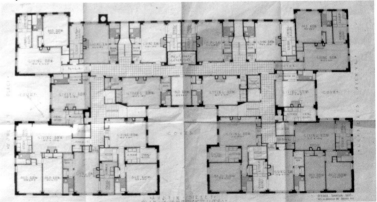

Kew Hall was the first major apartment building to go up in the heart of the new community. Covering over half a block, it followed the Dakota's plan (1883, on Manhattan's Upper West Side) of an interior garden court and multiple entrances from the court so there would be only two floor-through apartments per landing. That basic plan had been expanded and improved in a garden city manner by Edward MacDougall in Jackson Heights where the first true co-operative garden apartment complex, Linden Court, opened in 1920. Kew Hall followed two years later, with co-op ownership, automatic elevators (a high tech innovation that reduced labor costs), a garden court with a concierge's house (still extant) and a separate

Apartments by Rotholtz & Golden, 1922, at Metropolitan Avenue and Park Lane South, the Parc Chateau on Talbot Street, the Windsor Court at 83-19 116th Street and the Buckingham at 83-55 Lefferts Boulevard, among others, all have garden courts. Unlike the rigid geometry of their Manhattan predecessors, these buildings are irregularly shaped for better apartment layouts, while increasing land values pushed their height several floors beyond Kew Hall's five stories.

Other Kew Gardens sites for apartment buildings, however, were on narrow lots. To achieve their goals the designers drew up "pin-wheel" plans for their buildings, using irregular wings, sometimes an irregular "Y," sometimes an irregular "H," to ensure better apartment layouts with cross or corner ventilation, more sunlight and more privacy. The Kew Plaza, the Mowbray and the Shellball are all examples of these "pin-wheel" plans with belts of greensward encircling the building. Similarly planned buildings stretched along Lefferts Boulevard and Metropolitan Avenue. A modest bit of open land could be enough to give residents their bridge to nature. It could support a "forest" of trees that would eventually cloak the buildings or be cultivated as gardens for the delight of both residents and passers-by. At the Shellball, today's residents still use the back greensward as a vegetable garden; in the Kew Hall one section of the perimeter greensward is devoted to growing corn and tomatoes. At the rear of Hampton Court, abutting Forest Park, one of the residents has created a terraced garden-for-all-seasons in the tradition of the English country houses. If in some buildings the "greenbelt" has been sadly neglected or buried under poor landscaping, the land is still there and can be reclaimed for imaginative flower gardens or organic vegetable plots. This greenbelted land that encircles or penetrates the apartment buildings is as much a part of the community's heritage as the buildings themselves.

Yet all of this emphasis on nature did not negate the community's basic urban character. As the apartment towers rose, their silhouettes produced an urban skyline that delicately complemented the "natural" surroundings. Not tall enough to reduce the landscaping to penury as was the case in Manhattan, these Kew Gardens towers had presence enough to announce their urban mission. Kew Hall and the Kew Plaza, along with the Shellball and the Mowbray, were all grouped near or on Lefferts Boulevard, north of the railroad station. They created an urban ensemble of high rise picturesque massing while each maintained its own distinctiveness in silhouette, shape and decor, visually anchoring the northern edge of the "village."

Walk-up apartment houses

On the south side of the retail center, the Kew Corners apartment house at 120-32 83rd Avenue (originally, 151 Richmond Hill Avenue, 1925, Kieswetter & Hamburger) fulfills a similar mission of urbanity. Occupying a pivotal spot overlooking the village's "five corners" intersection (where Lefferts Boulevard, 83rd Avenue and Grenfell Street join together; some residents have dubbed it our "Etoile"), it was deftly designed in an almost Dutch Expressionist manner. Compact and only four stories high, each of its facades is differently treated to respect the different streetscapes: along commercial Lefferts Boulevard, a solid wall of shopfronts for urban presence; along 83rd Avenue, which is a leafy private house block, a generous greensward and the arched "porte cochere" to the interior court with its actual building entrances; and at the acute angle of the "five corners," a champfered corner, patterned brick and a Dutch Renaissance gable that anchors the southern end of the "village" and gives a charming vista to those passing over the Lefferts Boulevard "ponte vecchio." What continues the interest is knowing that the Kew Corners is a four-story walk-up whose three separate entrances, all from the inner leafy court, allow for two apartments per landing and floor-through layouts.

In our own time, walk-up apartment houses are considered a bit

Kew Corners Apartments, 120-32 83rd Avenue (121 Richmond Hill Avenue) at Lefferts Boulevard, at the "Five Corners." An excellent contextual building in the Dutch Colonial style that helps define the "village" center; its walk-up plan allowed for London-style floor-through flats.

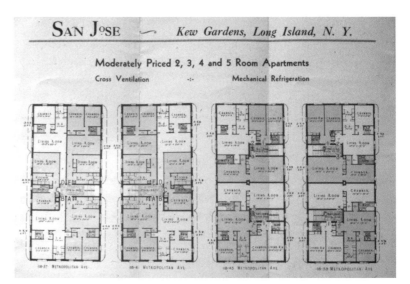

SAN JOSE — *Kew Gardens, Long Island, N. Y.*

Moderately Priced 2, 3, 4 and 5 Room Apartments

Cross Ventilation -:- Mechanical Refrigeration

Plan from original brochure, San Jose Apartments, 118-37 to 118-53 Metropolitan Avenue, 1928. Another example of walk-ups allowing for London style cross-ventilated flats in a variety of configurations; garden apartment planning for "a modest outlay of rent."

déclassé, as Americans prefer to be motorized whether they're travelling horizontally or vertically. But back in the 1920's, progressive architects like Clarence Stein considered the walk-up apartment inherently superior to its elevatored brethren. Stein, who with Henry Wright and Alexander Bing created Sunnyside Gardens in 1925, believed that the cost of elevators necessitated a single elevator bank and, therefore, a single entrance which in turn required interior public corridors. These corridors not only became dank and odoriferous but also led to "dead-end" apartments with only one exposure and poor ventilation and light. Walk-ups, on the other hand, allowed several entrances with individual stairwells, small landings at each floor and only two or three apartments per landing, mean-

ing corner exposures or floor-through plans. The Kew Corners is an example of that planning. Another example in Kew Gardens is the San Jose Apartments (1928) occupying four four-story buildings from 118-37 to 118-53 Metropolitan Avenue. The apartments were quite varied in layout, with floor-through one and two bedroom units. Yet the original brochure announces them as "really moderate priced suburban apartments" for those who want "a high-class suburban residential community" but who can only afford "a modest outlay for rent." The San Jose's amenities were certainly not those of Kew Hall or the Mowbray, yet both kinds of apartment buildings existed in this burgeoning new community. And all shared the same garden city ideals.

Towers-in-a-park

Other apartment complexes, away from the commercial center, were more resolutely "green" in their conception. The Beverly House (1938, Morris Rothstein & Sons), Beverly Road at Brevoort Street, sprawls like an irregular letter "Y" over its verdant corner site, its neo-Georgian porticoed main entrance set far back from Beverly Road to allow for a sweeping, tree-filled greensward.

At the other edge of the neighborhood is Hampton Court (1939; Park Lane South at Metropolitan Avenue), originally called Kent Manor, designed by garden apartment architect Benjamin Braunstein who had also done the Mowbray. On a large plot of land, which was to have been included in Forest Park, Braunstein created six free-standing neo-Georgian "manor" buildings each shaped in an irregular "H" and set in a lush English garden landscape that melds into the wooded hills of surrounding Forest Park. Yet Hampton

Hampton Court, Park Lane South and Metropolitan Avenue. The mixture of "city" and "country" that is typically Kew Gardens: six neo-Georgian "manor houses" rising from a lush natural landscape by a master of this genre.

Roof detail of Hampton Court (formerly Kent Manor), original brochure, Benjamin Braunstein, 1937. One of the finest garden apartment complexes in New York City, six neo-Georgian towers-in-a-park, not a parking lot. Forest Park, which surrounds Kent Manor, was "pulled" through the grounds.

A Kent Manor floor plan. Each "manor house" had a "pinwheel" plan for apartments that were well planned, well lit, private and swathed in greenery.

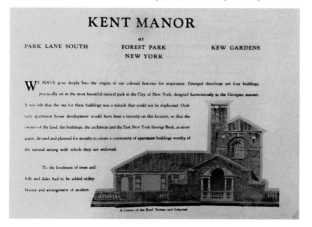

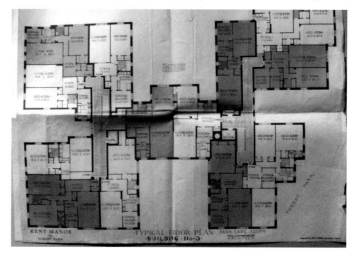

Court's neo-Georgian silhouette rises above the trees to create an urban skyline along both Metropolitan Avenue and Park Lane South. It's this constant interplay between urban forms and garden city ideals that is so intriguing, making Kew Gardens, like Jackson Heights and Sunnyside Gardens, an "urban" neighborhood visually as well as viscerally.

Architectural styles

The "architectural styles" chosen for the apartment towers were mostly variants of the Eclecticism the 1920's preferred: Tudor-Revival, Romanesque-Revival, Spanish Renaissance Revival or the more manorly neo-Georgian. The facades were considered stage sets for the street. Even though set back by front gardens from the sidewalk, Kew Gardens apartment towers define the streets, much like MacDougall's buildings in Jackson Heights, in the best urban tradition of the neo-classical city. Apartment houses frame the vista up Lefferts Boulevard towards the Maple Grove Cemetery Gate House; they also frame the straight slice of Metropolitan Avenue as it cuts through the neighborhood. Castle Court at 83-55 Lefferts Boulevard (between Metropolitan and 84th Avenues) sinuously frames the S-curve of the street, providing us with Tudor towers, turrets, details and a picturesque rounded corner at its southern end, demonstrating that architects once knew how to create streetscapes that were colorful, personable and unique.

The designers wanted their picturesque visual effects to create an "historic look." It's what gave the neighborhood then, and now, its charm and its architectural domesticity. The apartment buildings with their dark, rough-hewn tapestry brick (even if the building was steel-framed) and their slate-tiled roofs project the solid, traditional image of "hearth and home." Everything, including, ironically, the machine and modern mass production, was put to the service of creating this "look." All kinds of "hand-made" details were

Castle Court, tower vista, Lefferts Boulevard at 84th Avenue (St. Ann's Avenue). A Tudor Revival tower rises over ascending Lefferts Boulevard: our own Stirling Castle sitting on the highlands of Queens. The Beaux-Arts trained architects knew how to create a streetscape.

machine-made, often ordered from a catalogue: "stone" balconies made of terra cotta, Tudor "half-timbering" composite materials tacked on as a facade, "sculpted" gargoyles, urns and scrollwork of cast stone, and apartment house lobbies' "timber" beam ceilings and massive "stone" fireplaces of molded plaster-of-paris. But the end

Detail of the Mowbray, 1924. A triple-arched window with Corinthian columns, Colonial style window sash and terra cotta balcony (with its mysterious Papal symbolism) all set in a tapestry brick wall. These kinds of details, the frankly stage-set facade of a steel framed skyscraper, gave the neighborhood its unique visual character.

Detail of Kew Hall entrance, 83-09 Talbot Street, 1922. Tapestry or textured brick was used to give the apartment buildings an instant sense of history and longevity, a clever trick for a country as nomadic as the United States.

Kew Plaza, entrance to original Oriole Tea Room, 80-40 Lefferts Boulevard, 1924. A Tudor-Revival brick arch and adjoining wall grace Lefferts Boulevard opposite Talbot Street. Beaux-Arts architects always sought to make a vista "interesting" or "picturesque," making every street unique.

result was the impression of aged comfortableness and the mellowness that comes from tradition. We should remember today, as we replace original windows and other original elements, how important these details were to the cumulative ambiance of the neighborhood.

The apartment buildings set us another example. Though "skyscraper" in height, they mix effortlessly with the low-rise private houses that surround them. Even if some of the original homeowners might have disagreed, the '20's apartment buildings knew how to be good neighbors visually by sporting a "character" and a "charm" that allowed them to fit comfortably into the community's local landscape. They may have changed the scale of the neighborhood, but they did not destroy its essentially domestic character. Even at ten or twelve stories they maintained that distinctive "look."

Dale Gardens, an entrance, Robert Tappan, c. 1926. A brilliant piece of garden apartment planning by another master of the genre. Apartments masquerading as neo-Georgian townhouses encircled a verdant common that included a bubbling brook and Japanese-styled bridge.

Windsor Court, entrance, 83-19 116th Street, c. 1927. This Tudor Revival apartment house gives us a fieldstone and brick arch, picturesque chimney and tiled gables to delight the eye. When details like these are lost, the neighborhood is diminished.

Dale Gardens

There was one Kew Gardens apartment complex of the 1920s period that was purposely kept low-rise. It was designed as three- and four-story townhouses grouped around a verdant common that included picnic grounds, a playground and a small stream with a Japanese style bridge springing over it. Dale Gardens (c.1927) was designed by Robert Tappan, an interesting architect of the garden city generation. Besides Dale Gardens, he created Arbor and Forest Closes (1926-27) in Forest Hills, the English Gables retail complex (1925) in Jackson Heights and the delightful English styled semi-detached houses on 84th Street, also in Jackson Heights (1927). Dale Gardens, with its neo-Georgian detailing, floor-through layouts, entry to the houses only from the common, built-in garages and its small retail complex at one end, is itself worth studying and worth recognition. But in Kew Gardens it is simply another variant of this running theme: that apartment dwellers in the modern city need not sacrifice the privacy of their homes and the quality of their lives to live in an urban environment.

Kew Gardens apartment houses are a varied lot: low-rise or high-rise, walk-up or elevator, central courtyard, central common, or pin-wheel in layout, massive tower or charming "townhouses." All are coddled with verdant trees and threaded with gardens. These are apartment houses we can learn from. These are city dwellings, but done in a unique American fashion.

THE COMMERCIAL BUILDINGS

THE MAN BROTHERS obviously did not let any design detail of the new community escape their attention. In most New York City mid-rise neighborhoods the retail street is developed as an afterthought, with commercial buildings punched out from speculative designs. The "main street" is usually known more for its stores than for the design of its commercial facilities, rarely reflecting the style or ambiance of the residential neighborhood it serves. Kew Gardens is different.

Like Jackson Heights' 82nd Street and Forest Hills' Austin Street, Kew Gardens' retailing streets, Lefferts Boulevard and Metropolitan Avenue, reflect the community's specific character. The retailing development is not continuous, and although not all retail buildings are so sensitively designed, enough were given a Kew Gardens "personality" to achieve the desired effect.

The neo-Tudor style was the Mans' favorite retail style, a practice common in the suburban developments of the 1920's. Today, some people find the Tudor Revival towers, faux half-timbering and patterned brick work a bit too much like a Disney theme park, but the Mans' architects faced a problem that still puzzles the best of designers. In a brand new community, how do you give character to raw new buildings, especially in a residential community where creating "affective" architecture is very important? This is not an impersonal midtown commercial district, but a

The "Homestead" Building, retail and apartments, Lefferts Boulevard. at Cuthbert Road, 1914. The beginning of Kew Gardens' "downtown." A raw new community was made to feel like a timeless English village.

community that people call home. Home usually means roots and in a mobile country like ours, where roots are often stretched thin, it is even more important for our communities that their physical design convey a sense of "place" and "tradition." The neo-Tudor retail style gave residents an instant sense of history, as if these buildings had been lived in and shopped in over the course of generations.

"Main street" buildings

We don't know at this point all of the retail buildings the Mans actually built but we can be certain the neo-Tudor ones must have been by their hand or under their influence. Their basic "main street" commercial building contained stores at the street level and apartments above, a type of structure basic to "main streets" everywhere. Two such buildings, four-story in height, were built on Lefferts Boulevard north and south of the railroad line. The southern one at Cuthbert Road (1914; 81-37 to 81-45 Lefferts Boulevard) has housed the Homestead Delicatessen, a neighborhood institution, Koopmann's Florist Shop and Blendermann's Meat Market (now defunct). This block can be seen in a 1914 photograph that is one of the earliest views of the district and shows us the original design before part of it was remodelled in an *art moderne* style and the northern end demolished for a Beaux-Arts bank building that frames the "Etoile" intersection in the

Retail/apartment mixed use, Lefferts Boulevard and Austin Street adjacent to the LIRR station, 1925. The Mans practiced efficient planning by clustering the retailing and major apartment houses around the railroad station.

center of the village. The other "main street" type of structure went up at Austin Street (80-57 to 80-65 Lefferts Boulevard (1929, Martin, Harry & Wohl) where its four-story neo-Tudor silhouette plays off against the picturesque mass of the adjacent Shellball Apartments.

A more delicately scaled Tudor Revival two-story apartment and retail block was also built on Lefferts Boulevard opposite what was the Clubhouse, later the site of the Austin Theater. This Tudor-gabled building swings around the corner to Austin Street (80-60/80-64 Lefferts Boulevard and 82-60/82-74 Austin Street, 1925, Slee & Bryson), creating one of the more charming vistas of the neighborhood and serving as the main "backdrop" for the railroad station area. Though some details have been badly mangled in recent renovations, its neo-Tudor detailing, picturesque roofline and humane scale still securely anchors the northern end of the retail district. It was in one of these apartments, across the street from the Mowbray, that comedian Rodney Dangerfield spent his early days as just another local kid; another was the site of the infamous 1965 murder of Kitty Genovese.

The "ponte vecchio"

Along Lefferts Boulevard, spanning the LIRR tracks and furnishing the community with a core of retail storefronts is Kew Gardens' own modest but interesting "ponte vecchio" (nominated for listing in the National Register, 1993). It is probably one of several in the United States, but we don't know which others are extant. Its realization reveals the imaginative solutions, improvisational yet profitable, called up by the Man brothers in the evolution of their new community. It was not built until about 1930, almost twenty years after the community first began. Yet, when completed, it solved the urban planning problem of the railroad tracks cutting the center of "town" in two. The two sets of stores on either side of the street were probably built at different times because the western one has neo-Tudor detailing while the eastern side has a terra-cotta frieze in a modest Art Deco pattern. The engineering involved is more complex than we first might think, but ingenious in its solution to a thorny problem.

The "ponte vecchio" at Lefferts Boulevard, back view, c. 1930. This ingenious "bridge" of stores coalesced into Kew Gardens' village center. "Going to the village" to do shopping entered the neighborhood jargon..

The Kew Gardens "ponte vecchio" is actually three separate bridges. The Lefferts Boulevard bridge, bearing the street across the railroad tracks, was built in 1910 when the LIRR built its new main line. That bridge carried only the roadway across the tracks and is still standing, having been rebuilt in the early 1990's. The stores on either side have their own two separate bridges which went up, with the stores, in the early 1930's. However, these latter are not simple bridges with storefronts plunked down on them. Instead, the stores' principal bridges actually run through the "roofs" of the stores, not under their floors. The storefronts are then "hung" from the bridges like a curtain hanging from a curtain rod. A secondary bridge, under the storefronts, gives them something solid to rest on, but it is not the principal support for the stores. This complicated arrangement, using steel framing, was devised to use a medieval solution for a modern problem. In the original Ponte Vecchio in Florence, dating back to medieval times, the shops span water and only had to be pro-

tected against floods. In Kew Gardens, the stores are sitting over railroad tracks and must withstand the heavy vibrations of commuter rail traffic that roars past underneath. Therefore, this complicated arrangement of steel bridges was needed so the storefronts, hanging from their "curtain rod," would be flexible enough to withstand the daily rumblings of the trains. Medieval precedent plus modern technology produced a cohesive core of neighborhood shops. Thus, this extraordinary bridge served the commercial interests of the Mans and the railroad as well as the economic, social and esthetic needs of all Kew Gardens residents. Once both sides of the bridge had gone up, it was common for people in the neighborhood to say they were "going to the village" to shop; the "ponte vecchio" and its stores had become the heart of the community.

Other retail buildings

Further expansion of the retail district south along Lefferts Boulevard included a row of single story storefronts (c.1930) built over the front gardens of earlier Tudor Revival townhouses (c.1925; 81-53 to 81-69 Lefferts Boulevard) between Cuthbert and Beverly Roads. The neo-Tudor tourelles and crenellations of the storefronts, backed up by the march of solid brick chimney stacks rising from the houses, created a striking silhouette along Kew Gardens' main shopping street. Other neo-Tudor retail buildings include one at 81-64 to 81-74 Lefferts Boulevard, at Beverly Road; one at 119-01 Metropolitan Avenue, at Lefferts Boulevard; and a small scaled but handsomely detailed one at 116-02 to 116-10 Metropolitan Avenue.

Across Metropolitan Avenue from these latter storefronts is a more typical terra cotta commercial structure, 116-01 to 116-11 Metropolitan Avenue, at the corner of Audley Street, from probably the early 1930's. Handsome in its neo-Gothic, tan painted terra cotta detailing, it shouldn't be overlooked even though it doesn't conform to the neighborhood's more general Tudor Revival retail style.

Tudor Revival townhouses, c. 1920's, with Tudor storefronts, c. 1930's, built over the front gardens, Lefferts Boulevard/ Cuthbert to Beverly Roads. Brick chimney stacks, gabled roofs and half-timber framing rise above crenellated storefronts creating a distinctive streetscape along Lefferts Boulevard.

Tudor Revival commercial building, Lefferts Boulevard at Metropolitan Avenue, 1910's or 1920's. Kew Gardens' "main streets" are architecturally distinctive and instantly recognizable, a rarity among New York City neighborhoods.

Tudor Revival storefront, Metropolitan Avenue at 116th Street, 1910's or 1920's. Picturesque confection of fieldstone, tapestry brick, half-timbering and slate tile set at a distinct champfered angle designed by architects who knew what to do with a street corner.

Though both Lefferts Boulevard and Metropolitan Avenue are intraborough roads that run for miles, the passerby knows instantly where Kew Gardens sits along them. The retail streets are as visually distinctive as the rest of the neighborhood. Recent retail buildings have been less respectful. A new (1989) single-story commercial building at the corner of Lefferts Boulevard and Metropolitan Avenue is "dead" architecturally, although it occupies a key corner in the community. Its blandness, like tofu, picks up the taste of what's around it, but unlike tofu, this building gives nothing in return.

The "community" garage

Throughout the city, rather than allow cars to consume the landscape with their asphalt driveways and bulky single garages, garden styled complexes built "storage" for their residents' cars in clusters at the community's edge. Arbor and Forest Closes in Forest Hills grouped their cars in communal garages at the Queens Boulevard end of the property; Sunnyside Gardens had community garages built at the northern (LIRR yards) end of the development. Parkchester in the Bronx put its garages in a ring around the edge of the property and Roosevelt Island (1970's) built its common garage next to the bridge that serves as the community's vehicular entrance. This allowed for more terrain to remain gardens and greenbelts instead of parking lots, though in recent years, we have unfortunately seen more and more gardens everywhere replaced by black-top. Although Americans, even in the 1920's, expected their cars to be parked next to their living rooms, residents of garden communities obviously didn't mind a short walk to their automobiles.

Kew Gardens, built in the age of the automobile, as were the other garden community developments, tried to meet this new challenge. Kew Gardens' apartment houses, like those of Jackson Heights (Linden Court on 84th Street in Jackson Heights was the exception), were not built with garages.

Tudor Revival garage (presently the Chatillon scale factory) on Kew Gardens Road/83rd Drive (Kingsley Road) to 84th Avenue (Juno Road), 1920's. This was, most likely, the community's original garage, one of the more distinctive car storage facilities in New York City.

At first, only Dale Gardens provided its residents with on-site parking. Then Kew Gardens' first central garage was put up in the 1920's to solve that problem. An especially interesting commercial building, though today no longer serving its original function, the community's first central garage was built on land owned by the East Richmond Hill Land Company along Kew Gardens Road opposite Maple Grove Cemetery from 83rd Drive (then Kingsley) to 84th Avenue (then Juno).

It was a carefully detailed Tudor Revival structure that fit elegantly into the neighborhood, probably one of New York City's more handsome depositories for automobiles. We don't know if this garage was built exclusively for the residents of Kew Hall across the street or if it was open to the general public. After the Depression and War years, when the number of cars diminished, the garage was converted to other purposes.

The original neo-Tudor garage building still stands, rare if not unique in the city, beautifully maintained by the Chatillon Scale Company, its occupant for many years. It is worth noting that this factory takes greater pride in maintaining its "home" than many an apartment house owner in the neighborhood. Its neo-Tudor skyline complements its neighbors along this winding and woodsy stretch of Kew Gardens Road that borders Maple Grove Cemetery.

After World War II the need for a similar parking facility returned and a neo-Georgian garage, reflecting the change in architectural taste, was built along Kew Gardens Road, running from Lefferts Boulevard to 84th Drive, on the site of former greenhouses that had served the needs of Maple Grove Cemetery.

In 1994, this more recent garage was creatively converted to become the Early Childhood Annex to neighboring Public School 99, following a massive community effort to relieve school overcrowding.

Facing Maple Grove Cemetery, running west to east along Kew Gardens Road, we now have the new, still neo-Georgian Annex to Public School 99, the Chatillon Scale factory building, and then the rear of the Spanish Renaissance Revival Parc Chateau apartment house at 84-09 Talbot Street (c. 1928).

Further east, along the "S" curve of this old, hill-top road to Jamaica, the neo-Georgian silhouette of Dale Gardens completes the tranquil, picturesque vista. Together with the arching trees of Maple Grove Cemetery, the Victorian silhouette of the cemetery's Gate House and the neo-Colonial First Church, this stretch of Kew Gardens Road has a distinctive handsomeness that is worth noticing and worth preserving.

THE PUBLIC BUILDINGS

COMMUNITY'S WELL-BEING rests on schools and religious institutions and both were given a prominent position by the Man brothers on one of the community's highest hills.

The First Church

At Lefferts Boulevard and Kew Gardens Road, prominently located at the very crest of the hill, the First Church of Kew Gardens (1928) was built on land donated by the Mans. As in their earlier community, Richmond Hill, the Mans wanted solid community facilities that would attract the "right" kind of people to their new garden-styled "village." The church was designed in that Protestant style of large, clear windows, a light-filled meeting hall and a weather vaned spire that we Americans call Colonial. Originated by the English architects Christopher Wren in the late 17th century and James Gibbs in the early 18th,

P.S. 99, 1923-24, C.B.J. Snyder. Snyder was a brilliant architect who created a new standard for the city's public schools.

this is the style most expressive of the reformist ideals of American Protestantism. After a fling with neo-Gothic during the 19th century, American church builders returned to their roots. The First Church is a handsome example with marine glass windows (rather than the perfectly transparent glass of today) to convey the freshness of the newly minted Yankee religion of the 18th century. Hobart Upjohn, the architect, was the grandson of Richard Upjohn (Trinity Church on Lower Broadway) and is responsible for spartanly handled Colonial Revival churches including All Souls Unitarian Church (1932) on Lexington Avenue and 80th Street.

P.S. 99 and its Annex

P.S. 99, The Kew Gardens School, is a Collegiate-Gothic styled building constructed in 1923-24 diagonally across Kew Gardens Road from the First Church. It was designed by architect C. B. J. Snyder, one of New York's forgotten heroes. Practicing in the early 20th century, he specialized in public elementary and high schools, setting a standard for a new generation of school buildings. Planned to give their students the best setting for a good education, these buildings achieved their goals with functional layouts, high ceiling classrooms and huge windows for plenty of light, air and space. Also, this excellent interior

First Church of Kew Gardens, 1928, Hobart Upjohn; Lefferts Boulevard and Kew Gardens Road. Built on one of the community's highest hills formerly owned by Maple Grove Cemetery, it typified the type of community facilities encouraged by the Man family developers for their garden suburb "village."

planning was then wrapped in a simple neo-Gothic exterior that gave the building a feeling of dignity, a sense of the past and, hopefully, an aura of scholarliness. His most notable high schools, done in a neo-Gothic style, include Erasmus Hall High School (1903) in Flatbush and Flushing High School (1915) in Flushing. P.S. 99, with its large expanses of glass for brighter classrooms and its neo-Gothic trim to impress the eye and feed the imagination, shows us Snyder's work at its usual best.

A little known fact about P.S. 99's construction is that a private house, known as the Driscoll house (today's 82-46 Kew Gardens Road), once sat on the school's present site and had to be rolled on logs across the street to a new site in order to make way for the new building. The contractor who built the school and did the

move, George Driscoll, lived in the "rollable" house for the next fifty years.

In 1969, a modern wing was added to the 83rd Avenue side of the school along with a high-rise apartment tower, an Educational Construction Fund Project that underwrote school building expansions with air-rights development. Although only one-story in appearance, the new wing took advantage of the hill on which the school is situated; its oversized gymnasium and cafeteria were placed below or partially below ground.

The school's influence is more than architectural, as it is academically one of the City's prized elementary schools. Currently its student body represents some fifty different countries of origin and speaks thirty different languages. Its presence is an important magnet drawing young families to the neighborhood. In the 1990's, when overcrowding again threatened the school's quality of education, this politically active neighborhood petitioned to convert the 2-

The P.S. 99 Early Childhood Annex (1995; Michael Fieldman & Partners); Lefferts Boulevard and Kew Gardens Road. This 1952 neo-Georgian garage was sensitively converted into an Annex for P.S. 99 through the concerted efforts of a dedicated community.

story post World War II Georgian Revival parking garage (1952) at the corner of Lefferts Boulevard and Kew Gardens Road to an early childhood Annex for P.S. 99 (1995; Michael Fieldman & Partners).

The garage site had orginally been covered with large 19th century greenhouses providing flowers for the visitors to Maple Grove Cemetery. After World War II, when the locals began buying cars once again, and the original neo-Tudor garage a block away had been converted to other uses, the greenhouses made way for a neo-Georgian garage in red-brick with limestone trim and a coping punctuated with neo-classical globes. Even a lowly garage was given a first-class Beaux-Arts treatment by its original builders, probably due to its prominent location at this key intersection. One wonders today what new construction would be this respectful of the community and its visual character. Creatively transformed into the P.S. 99 Annex, the handsome if simple neo-classical building is helping to educate the next generation of New Yorkers.

These four buildings, the church, the school's Main Building, the 1880 Gate House for Maple Grove Cemetery and the 1951 Georgian Revival Annex form their own architectural cluster at the crest of this hill. Visually this picturesque cluster formed the northern boundary of the orignal community and today it serves as a gateway to the neighborhood for those arriving by the Subway. The spire and clock tower of the First Church and the Picturesque slate roof of the Gate House, the neo-Georgian detailing of the Annex and the neo-Gothic dignity of the school create a handsome ensemble of silhouettes. It was said, before buildings and tall trees blocked the view, that from the top of this rise one could see from Manhattan to the Hempstead Plain and from the islands of Jamaica Bay to the shores of Long Island Sound. This fine geographic setting, made convenient to "the city" by the electrification of the railroad, gave the Man brothers the confidence that their new community would succeed and for almost twenty-five years it did.

By the mid-1930's, with the simultaneous bankrupting of the

Maple Grove Cemetery Gate House and the First Church of Kew Gardens. On one of the area's highest hills, a picturesque cluster of public buildings includes the Colonial Revival First Church, the Victorian cemetery house, the neo-Gothic P.S. 99 and its neo-Georgian Annex. Today, this cluster serves as the community "gateway" to those arriving by Subway.

Mans, the building of the Subway, the ploughing through of the Parkway and the dramatic change in population, a whole new era began for Kew Gardens. But that could be the subject of another book. Here we wanted to spotlight the innovative family that created this community and give the Mans their due. Though we are not going any further into the post-Man history of Kew Gardens, we couldn't end a section on our neighborhood's public buildings without a nod to the Borough Hall complex that lies literally just on the other side of the hill.

Borough Hall and the Court House Complex

One of the three Art Moderne buildings in the community,

Adath Yeshurun Synogogue, 1948, at Lefferts Boulevard and Abingdon Road, one of the three Art Moderne additions to the post-Man community.

Queens Borough Hall, 1941, William Gehron and Andrew J. Thomas, Queens Boulevard at Union Turnpike.

Queens Borough Hall was built in 1941 by architects William Gehron and Andrew J. Thomas in a neo-Georgian version of a streamlined, very stripped-down late phase of Art Deco; the Austin Theater, John McNamara, 1936, and Adath Yeshurun Synogogue, 1948, both on Lefferts Boulevard, share in this Modernistic style. Moved from Jamaica as part of the government's efforts to decentralize its activities, Borough Hall was built along the old Hoffman Boulevard route of the 19th century in what was the southern end of the Flushing Meadows. Re-enforced by the Queens County Criminal Courts Building (Alfred Easton Poor and William Gehron, 1961); renovated and expanded (Ehrenkrantz & Eckstut, 1993), both buildings naturally have created their own civic center type neighborhood.

"Fat Boy"

And last, but never least, our community's own "David," our own Zeus, our very own Roman god: Civic Virtue, the statue of a muscle man in the throes of virile supremacy. Created in 1919 by neo-classical sculptor Frederick MacMonnies (1863-1937), the statue originally stood in City Hall Park where one expects it would be

The statue of Civic Virtue at its original location in City Hall Park, 1928.

appropriately at home. It is said that MacMonnies' model was an Irish New York City cop who had been, following a local tradition among Irish policemen on the force, an Olympic Games contender. The statue, in a typical posing of that time, which evokes cries of horror today, was of a male nude standing over two writhing females, the male representing civic virtue and the females civic vice.

When Fiorello LaGuardia became New York's mayor in 1934, he took an immediate dislike to the over-muscled Lothario whose bare backside faced LaGuardia whenever he left City Hall. Dubbing the statue "Fat Boy," he was only too glad to relegate it to Queens the year after Borough Hall opened. Today it stands in politically incorrect splendor unadmired by almost all; even the graffiti artists tend to ignore it. But we love it in spite of its faults, as it has become a beacon for guiding friends, guests and out-of-towners to that most important mixmaster to the world, the complex traffic configuration known as the Kew Gardens Interchange.

MacMonnies' controversial statue of Civic Virtue located today at the Queens Boulevard entrance to Kew Gardens.

EPILOGUE

THOUGH THE MANS WENT BANKRUPT and disappeared from the local scene after the mid-1930's, their legacy is still with us today. Primarily speculative developers, their hammering out a new kind of suburban development shows us what we Americans could have done in the Suburban Decades that followed World War II. Kew Gardens gives us planning principles and architectural solutions for an urban community including single family homes, high rise towers, retail complexes and public buildings that can still tell us something for our present age. It shows us that the American belief in living close to nature is not incompatible with city living and mass transit. It tells us that we don't have to pave over half of the country and that we don't have to consider the steering wheel our fifth limb simply to "pursue our happiness." Kew Gardens' noteworthy example rightfully belongs in the lexicons of our history as a sensible and humanistic way to urbanize the American landscape.

BIBLIOGRAPHY

Articles

"A Group of Buildings of Moderate Cost," *American Architect*, Vol. 132, No. 2524 (July-September, 1927), pp. 55-62. [#99 Newbold Place (82nd Road)].

Boyd, John Taylor Jr., "Garden Apartments in Cities," *Architectural Record*, Vol. 48, July-August 1920, pp 53-74 and pp 121-135.

Brown, Frank, "If You're Thinking of Living In: Kew Gardens," *The New York Times*, Real Estate Section, February 4, 1990.

Gottlieb, Jeff, "A History of Kew Gardens," six-part series, *The Leader Observer*, November 6, 1986*ff*.

Henao, Claudia, "History and Development of Forest Hills Gardens, Forest Hills, New York," *Columbia University Thesis*, Preservation Program, 1984.

Jackson, Kenneth T, *Crabgrass Frontier: The Suburbanization of the United States*. New York: Oxford University Press, 1985.

Long Island Railroad Company, *Suburban Long Island, The Sunrise Homeland*. New York: The Long Island Real Estate Board, 1922, Columbia University, Avery Library.

McAlester, Virginia and Lee, *A Field Guide to American Houses*. New York: Alfred A. Knopf, Inc., 1984.

Myers, Steven Lee, "Kew Gardens Sighs for Its Bridge of Stores," *The New York Times*, January 10, 1993, pp. 25, 27.

Queens Borough Chamber of Commerce, *Queens Borough, New York City, 1928*. Long Island City, The Tavern Topics Press, 1928.

Queens Borough, The Borough of Homes and Industry. New York: Queens Borough Chamber of Commerce, 1915.

"Recent Apartment Buildings," *Architectural Record*, vol. 63, March 1928, pp. 193-278.

"Richmond Hill and Kew Gardens," *The Brooklyn Daily Eagle*, September 8, 1910.

Thomas, Andrew J., "The Button Control Elevator in a New Type of Moderate-Price Apartment Buildings at Jackson Heights, New York City," *Architectural Record*, Vol. 51, May 1922, pp. 486-490.

Willensky, Elliot and White, Norval, "Kew Gardens," *AIA Guide to New York City*, Third Edition. New York: Harcourt Brace Jovanovich, 1988, pp. 760-762.

Willis, Walter I, comp., *Queens Borough, New York City, 1910-1920*. New York: Queens Borough Chamber of Commerce, 1920.

Maps *(in chronological order)*

Lands of Silas Butler: 1,032 Lots. Queens County Records: new map #2307; Vol. 7, Sheets 10-11. Filed April 2, 1835.

Atlas of Long Island, New York. Surveyed under the superintendence of F.W. Beers. New York: Beers Comstock and Cline, 1873.

Atlas of Queens County. Long Island, New York. Compiled under the direction of Chester Wolverton. New York: Chester Wolverton, 1891.

Queens Borough. New York: Sanborn Map Company:
    1901, Vol. 4, Sheet 125
    1902, Vol. 3, Sheets 119-120.

Atlas of the Borough of Queens, City of New York, Vol. 2. Compiled under the supervision of Hugo Ullitz, C.E. Brooklyn, N.Y.: E. Belcher Hyde, 1908.

Atlas of the City of New York, Borough of Queens, by George W. and Walter S. Bromley. Philadelphia: G.W. Bromley & Co., 1909.

"Eastern Part of Kew Gardens," Queens County Records: new map #1809. Filed August 11, 1911.

"Kew Gardens: Southern Part," Queens County Records: new map #2591, Book 21, leaf 50. Filed October 22, 1910.

"Holdings of the Richmond Hill Realty Company," Queens County Records: new map #968. Filed April 3, 1912.

"Holdings of the Kew Gardens Corporation," Queens County Records: new map #3428. Filed April 5, 1916.

Queens Borough. New York: Sanborn Map Company:
    1925, Vol. 6, Sheets: 1-3
    1927, Vol. 4, Sheets: 13-14
    1932, Vol. 20, Sheets: 77-78
    1935, Vol. 20, Sheets: 77-80.

National Register Nomination

"Ralph Bunche House," National Register nomination form, 1976.

Bibliography compiled by Harry Hansen

ACKNOWLEDGMENTS

OVER THE YEARS during which this publication has been a "work-in-progress" many sources contributed to its creation and I would like to acknowledge my deep indebtedness to them. Those in the forefront have been:

Harry Hansen, for his extensive research which has been blended into the text;

Jeff Gottlieb, President, Queens Historical Society and long-time friend of Kew Gardens, for the many old photos he made available;

Jeffrey Kroessler, architectural historian, who provided advice and moral support;

Jane Andrews, former resident of Kew Gardens, for interview material and her fine thesis on the American suburban house;

Alan Gowans, for his excellent book, *The Comfortable House,* that provides a fine appreciation of the post-1900 American suburban home;

Walter Eisenhardt of Kew Gardens, for the use of his family's archival material;

Queens Historical Society for the Thomas Hart Collection of original apartment house brochures;

Jae Yang, for her early creative layouts, and *Cooper Union,* for "loaning" her to us through one of their work-study programs;

Eitan Eadan of Kew Gardens for his help in gathering photographic surveys;

Carol Berger for her valuable critical comments and for the sustenance provided to keep the working staff at the computer;

Sylvia Hack for conceiving of the idea for the book and never letting us forget our objective;

Martin Hack and *Murray Berger* for all the innumerable hours they spent bringing this book to fruition.

Thanks to all of them---and to those I have overlooked.

BARRY LEWIS

ABOUT THE AUTHOR

BARRY LEWIS was born and raised in New York City and educated at the University of California at Berkeley, the New School for Social Research in New York and the Sorbonne in Paris.

Based in New York these last twenty-five years, he has lectured for institutions as diverse as the Cooper Hewitt Museum, the Bard Graduate Center, the University of Pennsylvania and the Harvard School of Planning.

He has written on "Midtown/Fifth Avenue" in the guide book, *New York Walks,* and wrote the "New York City Architecture" and "Borough of Queens" sections in the current *Berlitz Guide to New York*.

Currently, he teaches architectural and interior design history at the New York School of Interior Design. There he also conducts a course for the public, *The City Transformed*, on the history of New York City's architecture and urban planning, which is co-sponsored by Cooper Union and the New York Transit Museum.

Mr. Lewis has co-produced a series of short videos of historic New York neighborhoods, *City Close-Up*, shown on PBS Channel 13 in 1998/99. He has also appeared as the on-camera historian in Channel 13's acclaimed production, *A Walk Down 42nd Street with David Hartman* (Summer 1998).

Mr. Lewis has resided in Kew Gardens since 1970.